HIDDEN
BRITAIN

HIDDEN
BRITAIN

Tom Quinn • Photography by Chris Coe

NEW HOLLAND

This edition first published in 2008 by New Holland Publishers (UK) Ltd
London • Cape Town • Sydney • Auckland

www.newhollandpublishers.com

Garfield House, 86–88 Edgware Road, London W2 2EA, United Kingdom

80 McKenzie Street, Cape Town 8001, South Africa

Unit 1, 66 Gibbes Street, Chatswood, NSW 2067, Australia

218 Lake Road, Northcote, Auckland, New Zealand

10 9 8 7 6 5 4 3 2 1

ISBN 978 1 84773 129 6

Publishing Manager: Jo Hemmings
Senior Editor: Kate Michell
Copy-editor: Sue Viccars
Assistant Editor: Rose Hudson
Cover Design and Design: Gülen Shevki-Taylor
Cartographer: William Smuts
Production: Joan Woodroffe

Reproduction by Modern Age Repro Co Ltd, Hong Kong
Printed and bound by Kyodo Printing Co (Singapore) Pte Ltd

Photographs appearing on the preliminary pages are as follows:
Half-title page: The Apostles topiary at Packwood House.
Title page: Ancient woodland at Finchampstead Ridges.
Opposite page: Nelson's Tower at Forres is a curious octagonal memorial to the great naval commander.
Contents spread: Portmeirion, Castell Coch, Buxton Opera House and Blickling Hall are just four of Britain's most fascinating hidden gems.

CONTENTS

INTRODUCTION

When you look at Britain on a map of the world, it soon becomes apparent that, in terms of its physical size and location, the country is little more than a rather modest offshore island. Yet, for all its apparent insignificance, this small geographical area contains an extraordinary variety of landscapes: from the wild hills and fells of Scotland, the Lake District and Northumberland to the wide skies and ancient villages of East Anglia; from the tiny fishing villages and hidden beaches of Cornwall and Devon to the quiet downs and meadows of Kent and Sussex. Then there are rocky, wildlife-rich coastlines, mudflats and estuaries, lowland meadows and ancient farms, gin-clear chalk streams and broad, rain-fed rivers.

The rich diversity of this landscape is matched – if not exceeded – by the extraordinary architectural wealth of Britain's villages and towns. There is hardly a place in the entire country that does not contain something of interest: ancient abbeys, early almshouses and timber-framed cottages, magnificent country houses and castles, tiny churches and fortified manor houses.

Of course, much of England, Scotland and Wales is already well known. Visitors from both home and abroad discovered long ago the delights of Bath and Stonehenge, Burghley House and Westminster Abbey – and, indeed, of many less famous places – but the huge amount that remains to be explored is the main justification for this book. It is all too easy to miss the gems that hide behind the more obvious landmarks: places such as the Jew's House in Lincoln, which is the oldest domestic building in Britain; the historic semaphore tower at Chatley Heath in Surrey; the country's last remaining wooden Saxon church, tucked away in the Essex countryside at Greensted.

Away from these wonderful architectural survivals, often in the more remote corners of the countryside, can be found a wealth of stunning landscapes and habitats that are almost too numerous to mention: quiet hilltops, lush, secluded valleys and wide open fens.

This book could have been called 'Forgotten Britain', but the truth is that many of the places described here are not forgotten at all – or at least not entirely. Local people and those 'in the know' have long enjoyed the hidden gems on their doorsteps. No one, I'm sure, would be more delighted than they to know that with the publication of this book the places of which they are so proud will be enjoyed by a wider circle.

Right: Wade's Bridge crosses the River Tay in Aberfeldy and is a triumph of 18th-century engineering.

CORNWALL, DEVON & SOMERSET

The West Country has always been a place apart: from the wide, marshy landscape of the Somerset Levels to Cornwall's smugglers' coves, the far west of England has an atmosphere all its own characterized by ancient abbeys and lonely ruined tin mines, of isolated beaches and curious monuments.

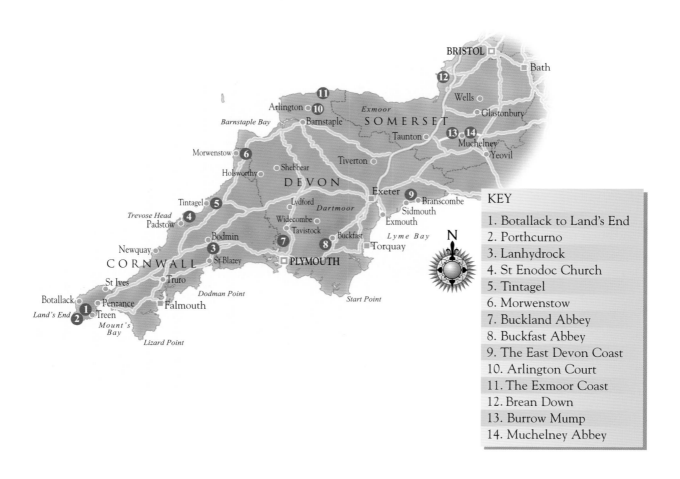

KEY

1. Botallack to Land's End
2. Porthcurno
3. Lanhydrock
4. St Enodoc Church
5. Tintagel
6. Morwenstow
7. Buckland Abbey
8. Buckfast Abbey
9. The East Devon Coast
10. Arlington Court
11. The Exmoor Coast
12. Brean Down
13. Burrow Mump
14. Muchelney Abbey

BOTALLACK TO LAND'S END

West Penwith, Cornwall

This beautiful and historic stretch of coastline deserves to be far better known. It begins a little to the north of St Just, near the village of Botallack – which was once an important tin-mining centre – and runs south towards Land's End, past rugged Cape Cornwall and along the golden sands of Whitesand Bay to Sennen Cove. On the coast nearby lies the machinery associated with the long-disused Crowns mine, whose atmospheric engine house clings precariously to the cliffs – it is surely only a matter of time before this impressive structure vanishes into the sea. All along this coast are similar echoes of the past in the form of more old engine houses; tall, dark chimneys and derelict buildings. These are the last visible remains of Cornwall's most famous industry, although below ground lie untold miles of forgotten and long closed tunnels.

Windswept and battered by gales, this stretch of coastline comprises an extraordinary mix of cliff, cove and headland, and the skies are filled with seabirds, such as fulmar, cormorant, shag, kittiwake and guillemot. Inland, the salt-spray-battered heathland provides a home for many unusual plants, including rock samphire and sea beet, thrift, sea campion and scurvy grass.

For the archaeology enthusiast, the field pattern a little inland is a source of endless wonder, for many of the field boundaries date back thousands of years; they are certainly pre-Christian, and in some places prehistoric. There is also a Bronze Age tomb at Carn

Above: The long disused Crowns tin mine is an atmospheric reminder of Cornwall's rich industrial past. It clings precariously to the cliff top, a monument to the tin-mining industry that was once widespread in this remote corner of south-west England.

Gloose, and Maen Castle Iron Age cliff-top fort is passed on the coast path between Sennen Cove and Land's End.

PORTHCURNO

West Penwith, Cornwall

Some 3 miles (5km) south-east of Land's End is the beautiful sandy beach of Porthcurno, overlooked by rugged cliffs on which stand the Logan Rock and the Iron Age Treryn Dinas coastal fort. Also just above the beach lies the extraordinary Minack Theatre, an amazing open-air venue hewn out of the cliff face, where you can watch a performance of Shakespeare accompanied by the sound of the waves hissing up the sands far below.

From Porthcurno you can walk along the coast path, either east to Penberth Cove or west to Gwennap Head. At Penberth Cove, small fishing boats are still launched from the secluded beach, providing a glimpse of Cornish life as it might have been a century or more ago. The Penberth Valley has remains of tiny meadows – or 'quillets' as they were known locally – where delicate flowers, such as violets, were once grown commercially.

At Porthcurno itself, there is the remarkable Museum of Submarine Telegraphy. Porthcurno was the location for the first submarine telegraph communications in the 1870s, when cables were laid under the beach and out to sea to the furthest corners of the British Empire. During the Second World War (1939–45), Porthcurno was a vitally important communications site for the whole country. Blast-proof doors lead to the wartime underground tunnels which now house vintage telegraph equipment dating back to the late 19th century.

Left: West Penwith encompasses some glorious coastal scenery and beaches. A walk along the coast path from Porthcurno is rewarded with this breathtaking view towards the rugged Logan Rock.

LANHYDROCK

Bodmin, Cornwall

During the middle decades of the 20th century, relics of the Victorian era became deeply unpopular. It is only recently, more than a century since the death of Queen Victoria in 1901, that the virtues of the late Victorian period have come to be recognized. One of the very best unspoiled examples of this period is Lanhydrock, a superb house that lies hidden away in the remote upper Fowey Valley amid 900 acres (365 hectares) of beautiful parkland.

The estate was bought in 1620 by an affluent local man, Sir Richard Robartes, and he set to work building a grand property on the land in 1630. The 17th-century house gradually decayed over the subsequent centuries until 1861 when Lord Robartes returned to his ancestral home from London. He employed the celebrated architect George Gilbert Scott, but 20 years after the house was rebuilt it burnt down.

The 17th-century gatehouse and north wing survived, but the rest had to be rebuilt. Richard Coad, a local architect, set to work on it in 1881, and no expense was spared. The house we see today is substantially as Coad left it – even the central heating system is Victorian!

The gardens are a delight, with superb collections of rhododendrons, camellias and magnolias in spring, and there are miles of footpath through the estate's beech woods and farmland, through which runs the River Fowey.

Above: The gatehouse at Lanhydrock is a splendid entrance to a most extraordinary house. Almost entirely a Victorian recreation, Lanhydrock, amazingly, still has its original central heating system.

St Enodoc Church

Daymer Bay, near Rock, Cornwall

St Enodoc Church was, for many years, quite literally buried in the sand, which may explain why it is relatively unknown today. It stands above Daymer Bay on a stretch of the Cornish coast that the late Poet Laureate Sir John Betjeman (1906–84) loved above all others, and he is buried here. Daymer Bay has a wealth of child-friendly rock pools and golden sand, and lies on the Camel estuary just south of the popular surfing centre of Polzeath.

The coastal path between Daymer Bay and Polzeath is – unlike most of the Cornish coast path – suitable for everyone, from the athletic to the less able. Yet it still offers fabulous scenery that nowhere else in the world can quite match.

St Enodoc Church, tucked away below Brea Hill, dates from the 12th century. When restoration work began in 1912 the area was all sand dunes and sand was piled so high round the building that it was almost impossible to get in. When the restorers finally cleared a path into the church they discovered the pews and other wood-work had turned green with mould, and £600 – which was a lot of money in those days – was spent on cleaning the place up and repairing the windows so that the sun could shine in once more.

The church's isolation from any village or hamlet is something of a mystery, and it may be that it was built – as many early churches were – on a site of pagan worship. The Christians were clearly intent on suppressing the old faiths – literally, as well as metaphorically.

Tintagel

Near Boscastle, Cornwall

Despite its famous links with the legendary King Arthur, Tintagel has been neglected in recent years by all except hard-line Arthurians. This is a huge pity because, quite apart from its historic associations, Tintagel has one of the world's most beautiful coastlines, with unrivalled views out across the Atlantic.

The ruins that can be seen today date only from the 13th century, when

Left: The small, simple and entirely unspoiled St Enodoc Church was Poet Laureate John Betjeman's favourite church. He was buried here in 1984, overlooking the landscape he loved.

Richard, Earl of Cornwall, refortified the site, long after Arthur is supposed to have departed from here for Avalon, his resting place. There are substantial castle ruins on the cliff edge and the remains of a medieval monastery on the adjoining island (the two are separated by a short bridge). Following recent archaeological finds of pottery fragments that have been traced to manufacturing centres in Spain, Tintagel is also now believed to have been a trading centre, linked to sites in the Mediterranean. Little has been found, however, to confirm any of the Arthurian tales. Nevertheless, this is a magical place, be it a bright summer's day or when the autumn mists roll in atmospherically off the sea.

Alfred, Lord Tennyson (1809–92) fuelled the Victorian enthusiasm for the legends of Arthur with his poem *The Idylls of the King*, which describes Merlin on the beach below the island. A number of visitors

Above: Tintagel has always been popular with fans of Arthurian legend, but the ruined castle and remote, beautiful countryside that look out across the Atlantic deserve wider recognition.

walking on the cliff top in the late evening have reported a ghostly presence, and, whether or not you believe the legends, it is easy to imagine the Knights of the Round Table striding across this remarkable part of the Cornish coast.

In Tintagel village there is a crooked, 14th-century slate-built manor house – known today as the Old Post Office – which has been beautifully restored by the National Trust. It became the letter-receiving office for this part of the county in 1844 following the introduction of the penny post. It's a gorgeous, picturesque little building, furnished with just the sort of crude, but rather lovely, rustic oak furniture it would have contained centuries ago.

MORWENSTOW

Near Bude, Cornwall

Morwenstow is a glorious, easily missed little hamlet just inside the Cornwall/Devon border. For centuries this region was inhabited by wreckers – those who lived by salvaging ships that foundered in the wild seas off the rugged coast. It has often been said that the law of salvage, which allowed goods to be taken by locals only if all those on board the ship had perished, led to dreadful acts of murder; in desperate times such acts were no doubt committed around Morwenstow. Today, those visitors who stumble across this delightful place come in search of the lovely walks along the cliffs or to explore the steep-sided combes and coves along this lonely and rugged coast.

This is the parish made famous by the Reverend Robert Stephen Hawker, incumbent at the church from 1834 to 1875. Hawker instigated the annual harvest festival ceremony that is still celebrated by most churches and church schools. He was also a poet and eccentric, who often clambered down the most dangerous cliffs to collect the bodies of drowned sailors to ensure they received a proper burial. Hawker had something of the hermit about him, and the tiny hut where he contemplated the world – and, no doubt, eternity – still exists. Parson Hawker wrote *Song of the Western Men*, the hymn that has become the Cornish anthem and which contains such stirring phrases as 'And shall Trelawny die? Then twenty thousand Cornishmen shall know the reason why.'

The Norman church is dedicated to the Cornish saint Morwenna and St John the Baptist. Just below the graveyard lies the vicarage (now privately owned). Hawker commissioned a local builder to create the vicarage's chimney stacks in the shapes of the various church towers he had encountered in his career!

Below: The vicarage at Morwenstow has an array of interesting chimney stacks, as commissioned by the eccentric Victorian incumbent, the Reverend Robert Stephen Hawker.

BUCKLAND ABBEY

Yelverton, Devon

Buckland Abbey is one of those rare and fabulous English houses that has fulfilled many roles over the centuries. It began life in the mid-1200s as a Cistercian monastery and eventually became the home of one of England's greatest seafarers – Sir Francis Drake (c. 1540–96).

In 1541, two years after the Dissolution of the Monasteries, Henry VIII sold the house to the well-established Cornish family of Sir Richard Grenville, who began the work of converting the monastic buildings. This scheme was more or less completed by his grandson, also Sir Richard. The second Sir Richard used the abbey as a house and inserted three floors into its huge vaulted interior – but the distinctive tower still reveals the building's origins. Sufficient space was left for a great hall, which has a fireplace dated 1576 and

Above: Buckland Abbey was the home of that great seafarer Sir Francis Drake (c. 1540–96), a man once so feared in Spain that Spanish children are still told that if they do not behave 'El Draco' will come and get them.

remains remarkably unaltered to this day.

The explorer Sir Francis Drake bought the house in 1580 and it remained in this seafaring family – two 18th-century Drakes were admirals – until the early 19th century.

Sir Francis Drake planned his defeat of the Spanish Armada in 1588 while at Buckland Abbey, so it is perhaps fitting that the abbey is now home to the Drake Naval, Folk and West Country Museum, with displays of medals from the time of the Armada as well as flags and other relics. Drake's own drum can still be seen in the house.

An original tithe barn – one of the largest surviving examples in the country at 160 feet (49 metres) long – stands just a few metres from the house.

BUCKFAST ABBEY

Buckfastleigh, Devon

Tucked away in Devon's beautiful Dart Valley, Buckfast Abbey was never a rich or famous monastic foundation. This may explain why parts of it have survived since the 12th century, unlike far better-known abbeys that vanished long ago. Buckfast – uniquely in England – was restored and is still used for the purpose for which it was originally built. Its history is fascinating.

The existing abbey church, vaguely Norman in style although built by the monks themselves at the end of the 19th century, follows precisely the outline of the long-vanished medieval abbey church and its high tower can be seen rising romantically through the surrounding woodland.

Originally founded in 1018, when Canute was on the English throne, Buckfast was dedicated to the rule of St Benedict, but by the mid-13th century the Cistercians held sway here. Archaeological evidence suggests that by the mid-14th century the monastic community had been badly hit by the plague and, with few monks to carry out repairs, many of the buildings were collapsing.

But fortune's wheel turned again, and by the mid-15th century the abbey was once again flourishing, though it never attracted large numbers of monks.

In 1539, monastic life at Buckfast and some 40 others like it in the West Country came to an abrupt halt thanks to Henry VIII and the Dissolution of the Monasteries. With the monks and their treasures gone, the buildings were plundered for stone or converted into farm buildings. Nevertheless, substantial if ruined parts of the original complex remained until 1800 when much of the site was flattened by its new owner, Samuel Berry, who kept only the Abbot's Tower and the 12th-century undercroft.

In 1882 another new owner, James Gale, decided to sell the

Left: Buckfast Abbey is the only religious foundation of its kind in England that is still used for its original purpose.

Opposite: The settlement of Branscombe lies a little inland from Branscombe Mouth, and retains a number of working historic buildings. The surrounding area is great rambling country.

site to a religious community, and by October 1882 monks were back at Buckfast after a break of more than 300 years. It took them a further 32 years to rebuild their church.

Today, Buckfast has an atmosphere and beauty more in keeping with religious sites in Catholic Europe than Protestant England, and as such it provides a remarkable glimpse back through the centuries to medieval times.

THE EAST DEVON COAST
Sidmouth to Branscombe, Devon

Despite the best efforts of modernizers and town planners, Sidmouth, splendidly situated in Lyme Bay, retains the air of a prosperous unspoiled Regency seaside town. It is awash with elaborate wrought-iron balconies, flower-filled gardens and stunningly beautiful houses. Landslips blocked up the town harbour centuries ago, and now the peaceful River Sid slides slowly into the sea over the pebbled beach.

The coast path between Sidmouth and Branscombe Mouth, to the east, provides spectacular views, lonely shingle beaches and some impressive gradients. From the top of Salcombe Hill there are fantastic views west across the town towards the Exe estuary. The path runs along the top of red sandstone Dunscombe Cliff before negotiating the deep, steep-sided combes leading to Salcombe Mouth, and later Weston Mouth. Finally, a steep drop leads to the beach at Branscombe Mouth.

The sprawling and ancient village of Branscombe, with its wealth of picturesque thatched cottages, 11th-century church and two good pubs, lies a little inland, and is said to be the longest village in the county. Branscombe has the air of a place forgotten by time.

ARLINGTON COURT
Near Barnstaple, Devon

The Devon architect Thomas Lee built Arlington Court in 1822 for Colonel John Chichester, whose family had owned the estate since the middle of the

14th century. But what is most remarkable about this house is that the rooms are almost exactly as Lee left them more than 150 years ago: each piece of furniture still sits in its original location, having been made specially for the house by a Barnstaple furniture maker.

Arlington Court also derives a special atmosphere from its extraordinary amount of clutter, most of which was collected by Miss Rosalie Chichester. She was born in the house in 1865 and lived there until her death in 1949. Miss Chichester – a relative of round-the-world sailor Sir Francis Chichester – collected vast numbers of model sailing ships, pictures of ships, shells, candle snuffers and much more.

Miss Chichester filled the house with caged birds, and allowed parrots to fly around at will. She introduced Shetland ponies and Jacob sheep to the grounds, and their descendants still roam there today. The house is now owned by the National Trust, whose wonderful collection of horse-drawn carriages is housed in the stable block.

The Exmoor Coast around the Heddon Valley

Near Combe Martin, Devon

If you want to explore this part of the North Devon coast, your best bet is to start at the Hunter's Inn, nestling at Heddon Gate in the bottom of the steep-sided and wooded Heddon Valley. The original thatched inn burnt down in 1895, and the present building dates from 1897. From here you can take a path beneath ancient oaks along the east bank of the River Heddon to find the shingle beach at Heddon's Mouth. Above the beach is a restored 19th-century limekiln: in earlier times lime was burnt in such structures in many parts of the country to produce cheap fertilizer. A walk east along the coast path towards Woody Bay passes along the cliff top near the Roman fort at Martinhoe, discovered as recently as 1960.

Much of the Heddon Valley and the surrounding area is owned by the National Trust and is designated as a Site of Special Scientific Interest. The almost primeval air of the valley woodlands is filled with birds, butterflies and other wildlife – here you may spot redstarts and warblers, pied flycatchers and tree creepers, foxes and deer.

The nearby Hangman Hills – also protected by the National Trust – can be reached either from the

Above: Walk eastwards along the Exmoor coast towards Woody Bay – seen here in all its summer glory – and you will pass a Roman fort which was discovered as recently as 1960.

Heddon Valley or from Combe Martin, 5 miles (8km) along the coast to the west. Climb Little Hangman (700 feet/214 metres) then continue along the coastal path to Great Hangman (1043 feet/318 metres), the highest cliff in southern England and home to rare falcons, moths and butterflies, as well as guillemots, razorbills and kittiwakes.

BREAN DOWN

Brean, near Weston-super-Mare, Somerset

Brean Down is a spectacular limestone peninsula that runs 1½ miles (2.4km) out into the Bristol Channel at the western end of the Mendip Hills. Formerly an island, it is connected to the mainland by a 900-yard (1000-metre) strip of salt marsh. The peninsula is bordered by steep cliffs and a rocky foreshore, and is both a Site of Special Scientific Interest and a scheduled ancient monument. With wide views, fascinating archaeology and absorbing geology and wildlife, Brean Down is unique, its value only enhanced by the fact that so few people visit it.

At the extreme seaward end of the down lies Palmerston Fort, built in 1865 and adapted and reused in the Second World War (1939–45), and now – like Brean Down itself – looked after by the National Trust. The great radio pioneer Guglielmo Marconi carried out a number of experiments here in 1897, transmitting and receiving radio signals across the Bristol Channel.

their first landfall here; resident birds include oystercatcher and dunlin. Among the plants are rock samphire and sea lavender, white rockrose and Somerset hairgrass. The open grassland is home to delicate chalk blue and dark green fritillary butterflies.

BURROW MUMP
Isle of Athelney, Somerset

The Somerset Levels once comprised hundreds of acres of waterlogged swamp, supporting wildfowl and wading birds and inhabited by isolated groups of hardy individuals. The latter eked out a living by weaving baskets from the willows that grow abundantly in the area, trapping birds and catching eels and other fish. Much of the Levels region has been drained, but the flat landscape – reminiscent of the East Anglian fens – retains something of its ancient atmosphere.

Rising out of this wide, flat, wet landscape is a solitary hill known as Burrow Mump. At the top of the hill is a ruined church. It was to here, at the

Brean Down has been inhabited for thousands of years: there are Bronze Age barrows and Iron Age field systems as well as early Christian remains and a Roman temple. The ancient peoples may have long gone, but a rich diversity of wildlife remains. Many migrant birds – including brambling, redpoll and red bunting – make

height of the English Civil War in July 1645 that the defeated remnants of King Charles I's army retreated after the nearby Battle of Langport. They were pursued by the Roundheads and finally routed.

The church on the mump had long fallen into disrepair when a 19th-century local landowner decided it would make an attractive 'folly ruin', in line with the fashion of the 18th and 19th centuries.

Burrow Mump has been owned by the National Trust for more than half a century, and there is no doubt that it is a very special place indeed. It has associations with nearby Athelney, where King Alfred (849–99) is said to have held court, and it offers the most glorious views across the Levels from its summit. Glastonbury Tor can be seen some 10 miles (16km) away and when the weather is fine you can spot the tower atop the Tor, which is all that remains of the 15th-century church of St Michael.

MUCHELNEY ABBEY

Muchelney, Somerset

Founded by Ine, a 7th-century King of Wessex, the monastery at Muchelney was destroyed in Viking raids and then rebuilt in the 10th century. The Dissolution of the Monasteries in the 16th century resulted in the destruction of this beautifully situated Benedictine foundation, but the ground plan, cloisters and abbot's house survived.

Most of the monastic structures were plundered for building materials and the abbot's house was reused as a farmhouse. Both the cloisters and the abbot's house have been restored. The abbot's house is now open to the public and provides a rare glimpse of the pre-Reformation world of monks and cloisters.

Muchelney means 'big island' and when flooding occurs the site becomes cut off, as it must have been over a thousand years ago before the monks drained the land and built their carp ponds and closed communities.

Below: The ceiling at Muchelney Abbey's abbot's house is lavishly and intricately decorated. This building survived the destruction of the 16th-century Reformation intact, finding a new use as a farmhouse. Now restored, it provides a unique glimpse into the distant past.

Dorset, Wiltshire & Hampshire

Hills and headlands, pretty medieval villages and Iron Age hill forts typify this much-visited part of the country. But away from the best-known places there is plenty to discover down narrow lanes and over the wide and windswept downlands.

KEY

1. Golden Cap
2. Eggardon Hill
3. The Smith's Arms
4. St Laurence's Church
5. The Peto Garden
6. Caen Hill Locks
7. Silbury Hill
8. Cherhill Down
9. Maud Heath's Causeway
10. Malmesbury Abbey
11. North Meadow
12. Pepperbox Hill
13. Mottisfont Abbey
14. Bembridge and Culver Downs

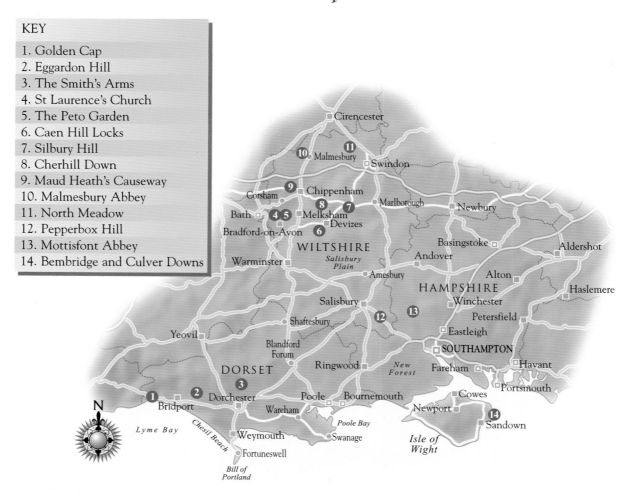

GOLDEN CAP

Near Bridport, Dorset

Far less well known than other stretches of cliff face, such as Beachy Head in Sussex, Golden Cap (at 626 feet/191 metres above sea level) is the highest point on the south coast. It is hemmed in on either side by the debris of massive cliff erosion. The huge areas of collapsed cliff face beneath the Cap – now inaccessible and therefore free of human interference – have become a haven for numerous wildlife species: everything from newts, toads, badgers and slow worms to rare birds of prey, foxes and several species of deer. At the bottom of the cliff is a band of blue lias rock, rich in fossil remains, and above that lies the golden gravel from which the Cap takes its name.

The view from Golden Cap across these wildlife sanctuaries and out to sea is breathtaking. There are treasures just inland, too: head down the western slope of the Cap to reach the little stream known as St Gabriel's Water. A little way upstream may be found the tranquil ruins of 13th-century St Gabriel's Church. St Gabriel's Water tumbles into the sea at a shingle

Above: The beach at Golden Cap features large areas of collapsed cliff which provide a haven for wildlife – mainly because they are inaccessible to humans.

beach, so secluded that it was for centuries a favourite landing place for smugglers of contraband goods, such as brandy from France.

Golden Cap is part of a large tract of land owned by the National Trust, and the area has almost 18 miles (30km) of footpath, so it's a place to enjoy at your leisure.

EGGARDON HILL

Bridport, Dorset

Windswept and lonely even today, Eggardon must have been an awe-inspiring place when its hill fort was constructed above the endless bear- and wolf-inhabited forest that completely covered the lowlands and valleys.

The Iron Age fort – which covers an impressive 40 acres (16 hectares) – still has its magnificent ramparts and ditches, and almost certainly preserves, deep beneath the soil, some splendid archaeological riches; the site has not been excavated in modern times. Thomas Hardy called the hill 'Haggardon' in his novel *The Trumpet Major*, and it is as bleak and beautiful as any of the author's greatest works. On a clear day you can see the sea to the south and, to the north-west, Dorset's highest hill – Pilsdon Pen, rising to 908 feet (277m), and with its own Iron Age fort.

THE SMITH'S ARMS

Godmanstone, Dorset

Arguments about which establishment is truly entitled to the accolade 'Britain's smallest pub' are unlikely ever to be settled to everyone's satisfaction, but among the several claimants to this title is the Smith's Arms, which measures just 20 feet by 10 feet (6 metres by 3 metres).

This tiny, crooked thatched house dates from at least the 15th century, but may well be even older. Legend has it that it was once the village blacksmith's shop, and that Charles II (1630–85), famously fond of a drink, found

Below: The Smith's Arms in Godmanstone, Dorset, claims to be England's smallest pub. It is certainly one of the oldest in the country, and oozes character and history.

just what he needed here when passing through the village. So pleased was he that he promptly granted the owner permission to sell drink to a wider public, which is precisely what's been happening ever since.

ST LAURENCE'S CHURCH

Bradford-on-Avon, Wiltshire

Debate rages as to the exact construction date of this extraordinary little church which, until relatively recently, was thought to be just another old house! Stylistically it looks as though it was built in the early 11th century, but other evidence – most notably written – suggests it was in the 8th century.

St Laurence's is very lucky to be still standing, at any rate. It probably ceased to be used as a church in the later Middle Ages, and certainly by the early 18th century the nave was being used as a school, while the chancel had been converted into a house, with two floors inserted in its tall frame.

Canon Jones, the local vicar, began to investigate the buildings in the 1850s. From his researches – particularly a reference in William of Malmesbury's *Gesta Pontificum* of 1125 – Jones concluded that this altered building was actually extremely ancient. William

had described how 'to this day there exists a little church which Aldhelm caused to have built to the name of the most blessed St Laurence'. Canon Jones pressed for the return of the church to ecclesiastical use and in 1871 it was bought by the Church Commissioners and reconsecrated to St Laurence.

Typically for Saxon buildings – St Laurence is rather tall in relation to its ground dimensions. It has a small nave and a tiny eastern chancel, with an archway between. Two angels – dated to *c.* AD 950 – have been carved on either side of the arch. Originally built without windows (these were added towards the end of the Saxon era) the church has distinctive arcading and reeded pilasters.

THE PETO GARDEN

Iford Manor, Bradford-on-Avon, Wiltshire

Harold Peto, of Huguenot descent and an architect by profession, created this extraordinary Italianate garden between 1899 and 1933. Its significance can be judged by the fact that it is listed Grade 1 by English Heritage. It is a romantic garden, built to reflect the sunny hillside gardens typical of Italy: there are terraces, ponds, broad walks, little groups of mature trees and sculpture (much of it collected on Peto's travels) and wonderful views across the countryside.

The 2½-acre (1-hectare) garden includes the loggia, the great terrace and the cloisters – a building in which operas are performed each summer. The garden contains many specimens that have survived from Peto's own first planting scheme, such as wisteria, cypresses and scented lilies.

The house that is attached to the garden – Iford Manor – is almost as interesting: although medieval in

Above: St Laurence's Church dates from well before the Norman Conquest. The evidence of Saxon craftsmanship here is overwhelming and the church contains some fine 10th-century carvings.

origin, it has, like so many English country houses, a classical façade which was added in the 18th century.

The general view among Peto's professional admirers seems to be that he combined the formal and the informal brilliantly in this unique garden, which should be on every tourist's list of places to visit.

CAEN HILL LOCKS

Devizes, Wiltshire

This extraordinary example of Georgian engineering was completed in 1810 as part of the final section of the 87-mile (140-km) Kennet and Avon Canal.

John Rennie, the engineer, decided that the only way to get the canal (which linked Bath and Reading) round Devizes was by running it up the side of a hill! But he was faced with a huge problem: the usual system of a flight of locks, with a lock, then a basin, then a lock, and so on, immediately above each other, was not possible, as too many 'steps' were needed to negotiate the steep gradient of the hill. Rennie, therefore, had the brilliant idea of building basins at the sides of the flight which would hold enough water to enable the locks – which needed to be situated very close together – to work. These side basins can still be seen today.

It took 29 locks in all to climb 2½ miles (4.25km) up the hill, with the spectacular Caen Hill flight of 16 locks being central to this great feat of engineering.

This part of the Kennet and Avon Canal was still in use until just before the Second World War (1939–45). It soon became derelict and it was only after a lengthy period of massive restoration that the locks were returned to full working order; they reopened in 1990.

SILBURY HILL

Near Marlborough, Wiltshire

Silbury Hill is one of the strangest structures in the world – and structure it is, despite its appearance. This tall, conical, grass-covered hill is entirely man-made, and we have no real idea why it is there.

The effort involved in building it, without the help of modern tools, must have been prodigious. Undamaged – despite the passage of more than three thousand years since its construction – the hill stands in the middle of the Wiltshire Plain near Marlborough. It is estimated that the amount of soil and rubble moved to make it rivals

Left: A great engineering feat of the canal age, Caen Hill Locks draw water up a hill that must have seemed insurmountable to those who first hoped to connect Bath to Reading by the Kennet and Avon Canal.

the amount moved to create the Great Pyramid at Giza in Egypt; one estimate reckons that 500 men working continuously seven days a week for 15 years could only just have completed the work.

It's been said that the mound was a colossal grave for a great Neolithic king, but no archaeological evidence of burial has been found; others claim the hill is some kind of a sundial or zodiacal indicator, but again there is no real evidence.

It has, however, been ascertained from archaeological investigation that Silbury Hill began life as a 20-foot (6-metre) mound, which was later capped with chalk rubble. Later it was increased in height dramatically to its present 130 feet (40 metres) by the digging out of a 25-foot deep (7.5-metre) ditch round its base, and the addition of the excavated material to the top. The hill now covers just over 5½ acres (2.25 hectares) of ground.

Below: Silbury Hill was a mammoth feat of engineering when it was completed more than 3000 years ago by a people whose intentions remain utterly obscure.

CHERHILL DOWN
Near Calne, Wiltshire

Above: Cherhill Down, with its chalk horse, provides wonderful views across the Wiltshire plain and is topped by the splendid monument to William Petty (1623–87), Surgeon General to Oliver Cromwell (1599–1658).

Cherhill Down rises high above the rolling Wiltshire Plain and is topped by the splendid 125-foot (38-metre) Lansdowne Monument, a stone obelisk built in 1845. Designed by Sir Charles Barry on behalf of the third Marquis of Lansdowne, the monument commemorates Sir William Petty. Petty rose from humble beginnings to become Surgeon General to Oliver Cromwell and one of the wealthiest men in England. His daughter married the son of the third Marquis.

Below the monument lie the remains of an Iron Age hill fort known as Oldbury Castle, and on the slopes of the hill – which is now looked after by the National Trust – can be found one of Wiltshire's wonderful white horses, carved out of the underlying chalk. This horse dates from 1780 and was created by Dr Christopher – 'Mad Doctor' – Alsop of Calne. Alsop was a friend of the great equestrian artist William Stubbs. He is said to have directed the cutting of his horse by bellowing instructions through an early megaphone; this and other eccentricities earned him the 'Mad Doctor' title! The horse originally had a glass eye made from upturned beer bottles.

Maud Heath's Causeway
Near Chippenham, Wiltshire

Maud Heath was an extraordinary woman who decided in 1474 to finance the building and future maintenance of a good solid path from the village of East Tytherton, where she lived, to Chippenham, the nearest market town. Much of the land along the route was low-lying and flooded regularly in the Middle Ages, rendering the route difficult, especially in winter. Maud wanted to make sure the country people – and particularly those of her village – could walk comfortably and dry-shod to the town, and so spent a colossal sum on the raised pathway that survives to this day.

The causeway runs from Wick Hill through East

Above: After the passing of more than five centuries, much of the remarkable causeway built by Maud Heath between East Tytherton and Chippenham is still visible, particularly at the Kellaways section, seen here. The money Maud left in trust is still used for annual maintenance work on the causeway.

Tytherton, crosses the Kennet and Avon Canal (built in the early 19th century) and the River Avon, then runs on past Langley Burrell to Chippenham.

For much of its length the causeway is now just a raised path, but the section at Kellaways (as pictured above), which was rebuilt early in the 19th century, shows how it must once have looked throughout its length. It stands around 5 feet (1.5 metres) high, and was originally supported by 64 brick arches. The causeway is still maintained by a committee of trustees which has met every year since Maud Heath's death. Maud had sufficient presence of mind to leave money for maintaining the causeway, and even today the Trust's investments are now worth around £100,000 a year. A pillar placed at the river crossing at Kellaways in 1698 details the story, and there is a Georgian statue of Maud, dressed in bonnet and shawl, at Wick Hill.

MALMESBURY ABBEY
Malmesbury, Wiltshire

The mostly 12th-century remains of this once remote abbey represent approximately a third of the original buildings, but given the havoc wreaked during the Dissolution of the Monasteries in the 16th century, it is remarkable that even this much survives.

The abbey church originally had a spire taller than that of Salisbury Cathedral, but the spire collapsed early in the 16th century. When Henry VIII closed all the monasteries, a local man – one William Stump – bought what remained at Malmesbury and decided to convert it into the parish church, so ensuring the survival of this wonderful building.

Malmesbury is said to be the place where the Cotswolds meet the West Country, and its former importance can be judged by the fact that Athelstan (895–939), the first king of a united England, is buried at the abbey. The mid-12th-century south porch – through which visitors enter today – is a splendid piece of Norman work, and there is a superb vaulted roof above the nave.

NORTH MEADOW
Cricklade, Wiltshire

Cricklade is an ancient village – archaeologists have found evidence of a Saxon mint here, along with Roman remains. The village lies on the banks of the infant River Thames, and was busy and prosperous during the Middle Ages. At the north end of the High Street, just by the old stone bridge over the Thames, is the extremely rare habitat known as North Meadow. Most of lowland Britain's water meadows have been ploughed up for agricultural purposes, but odd

pockets remain here and there, saved only by the efforts of a concerned minority. North Meadow, or Nar Mead as it is known locally, is one such pocket.

In spring and summer it is a mass of rare and beautiful flowers, including the snake's head fritillary, which blooms in April. Such rarities explain why the meadow has been a designated nature reserve since 1973. Its 112 acres (45 hectares) have never been sprayed with modern chemicals, nor ploughed or damaged in any way.

In medieval and earlier times, 'right holders' in the village could graze their animals on the mead between 12 August and 12 February. The meadow is in fact old church 'lammas' land ('lammas' means harvest festival, the name being derived from 'loaf mass').

Above: No one really knows why the 17th-century octagonal folly on Pepperbox Hill was built, but one theory suggests that it was to allow the wives of local landowners to watch the progress of the hunt without being seen themselves.

Opposite: A substantial chunk of Malmesbury Abbey, where the great Saxon king Athelstan was buried in 939, survives because it was converted into the parish church.

PEPPERBOX HILL
Near Salisbury, Wiltshire

An octagonal three-storey brick tower that looks rather like a pepperpot, the Pepperbox sits high on Brickworth Down, commanding wide views both east and west.

Sir Giles Eyre built the folly in 1606 for reasons that remain obscure. One suggestion is that it was a place from which local landowners' wives could watch the hunt without exposing themselves to the public gaze.

Pepperbox Hill enjoyed its greatest fame – or notoriety – in the early 18th century when it was apparently a haunt of highwaymen. These scoundrels would attack carriages as they reached the top of the hill where the carriages and their occupants were vulnerable because the horses were supposedly too tired after the climb to gallop away!

Apart from the Pepperbox, the hill is notable for a series of communication experiments carried out here by Guglielmo Marconi in 1896. During one such experiment, Marconi managed to send a signal to Pepperbox Hill from over 4 miles (6km) away; the rest, as they say, is history.

MOTTISFONT ABBEY
Near Romsey, Hampshire

Mottisfont Abbey was built originally as an Augustinian priory and is now one of those ruined monasteries that has, over the centuries, taken on a wonderfully romantic air. Mottisfont's special and modern-day secret is that it is home to the national collection of old-fashioned roses, which look divine and smell like heaven. These can be enjoyed in the gardens, which are also resplendent with mature trees – including the biggest plane tree in the country – and perfect green lawns that run down to a classic English river.

Mottisfont was built in meadowland by what is now the most famous chalk stream in the world – the River Test. Despite being less than two hours' drive from London, the Test has all the appearance of a pristine, entirely unpolluted stream. The abbey took its name from a spring that fed

Left: The classical splendours of Mottisfont Abbey are just one aspect of a wonderful estate that began life as an Augustinian priory.

the Test here ('font' meaning 'spring'). At the Dissolution in 1539 – as with many monasteries – Henry VIII simply gave Mottisfont to a friend: the recipient in this case was his Lord Chamberlain, William Sandys, who exchanged the villages of Chelsea and Paddington for the abbey and its land. Bizarrely, Sandys demolished the residential parts of the monastery and converted the nave and tower of the church into his new house.

Inside the house is found Mottisfont Abbey's other great secret: the magnificent drawing-room mural by the American artist Rex Whistler (1834–1903). The wall painting (Whistler's last work) is a superb example of *trompe l'oeil* – a technique that gives the impression of three-dimensional reality. Whistler's subject is a sort of Gothic extravaganza of pillars and pelmets.

BEMBRIDGE AND CULVER DOWNS
Isle of Wight

Bembridge and Culver Downs give you the sense of being on top of the world as you gaze across the Solent (provided the weather is clear!) towards Portsmouth and the North Downs beyond. Compared to the tea shops and towns that attract most of the tourists to the Isle of Wight, the Bembridge and Culver Downs are relatively little visited – a great pity, given the fabulous sense of space they provide. The Victorian Poet Laureate Alfred, Lord Tennyson (1809–92), who loved these downs and lived nearby for many years, thought this the best air in the world. It was, he said, 'like champagne'.

If you walk the 5 miles (8km) from Bembridge to Sandown via Bembridge Down and Culver Cliffs, you will see all that this spectacular part of the country has to offer.

Owned by the National Trust, Bembridge and Culver Downs are part of a chalk headland that juts out to sea at the eastern end of cliffs that run all the way along the south coast of the Isle of Wight to The Needles, at the island's western tip.

At Bembridge there is the island's last remaining windmill. Built around 1700 (and only recently restored), it has most of its original wooden gear; the care and skill of the joiners and carpenters who put it together is a revelation. The village's Maritime Museum and Shipwreck Centre has a fascinating collection of artefacts, including a 70-year-old jar of rum that was salvaged from a wreck.

Below: Bembridge and Culver Downs were the haunt of the Victorian poet laureate Alfred, Lord Tennyson (1809–92), who lived nearby for many years. He is reported to have said of the air on the downs that it was 'like champagne'.

WORCESTERSHIRE, HEREFORDSHIRE, GLOUCESTERSHIRE, WARWICKSHIRE & OXFORDSHIRE

These ancient counties take us to the very heart of England, to a land of ancient timber-framed houses, wildlife-rich hills and great estates tucked away in secret valleys.

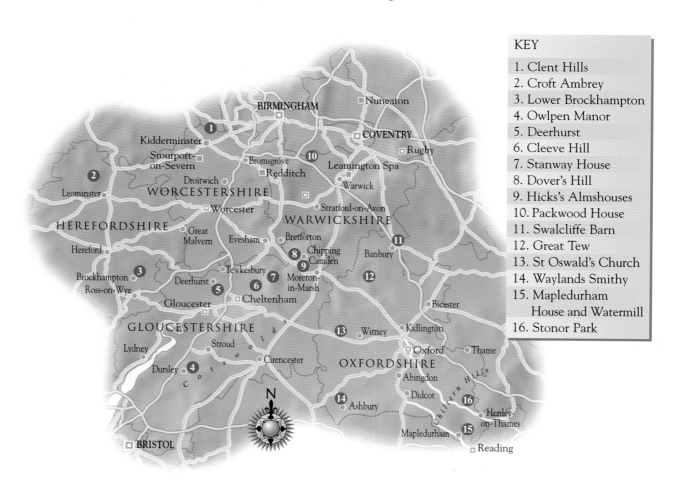

KEY

1. Clent Hills
2. Croft Ambrey
3. Lower Brockhampton
4. Owlpen Manor
5. Deerhurst
6. Cleeve Hill
7. Stanway House
8. Dover's Hill
9. Hicks's Almshouses
10. Packwood House
11. Swalcliffe Barn
12. Great Tew
13. St Oswald's Church
14. Waylands Smithy
15. Mapledurham House and Watermill
16. Stonor Park

CLENT HILLS

Near Stourbridge, Worcestershire

This beautiful landscape deserves to be as popular as the South Downs or the Peak District. At roughly 1000 feet (305 metres) above sea level, the summit offers wonderful views: to the west over the Worcestershire Plain and Severn Valley towards Wales, and east over the Midlands, the Black Country and Birmingham. At the highest point there is a group of four standing stones. This may look like a Neolithic or Bronze Age monument, but don't be fooled – the stones were actually placed here in the 18th century as a kind of folly, a self-conscious effort in antiquarianism!

The Clent Hills are made up of three sandstone ridges with scattered groups of pollarded beeches and small clumps of Scots pine. There is also an arboretum, and remnants of the original heathland. Among the rare plants that grow in quiet undisturbed corners are bird's-foot trefoil and cuckoo flower.

The hills are crossed by many footpaths and bridleways. In the 19th century the area was particularly popular with day-trippers from the then gloomy industrial Midlands.

Below: From the top of the Clent Hills, where clumps of Scots pine dot the ridge, you can see both west over the Worcestershire Plain and Severn Valley towards Wales and east over the Black Country and Birmingham.

CROFT AMBREY

Near Leominster, Herefordshire

A hill community lived in Croft Ambrey for more than a thousand years, from about 1100 BC to roughly AD 50. What began life as a triangular-shaped Iron Age hill fort was extended over the centuries, most notably in about 390 BC when archaeological evidence suggests that it was expanded from a little over 2 acres (less than 1 hectare) to cover 5 acres (more than 2 hectares); rows of huts were built and massive ramparts added. Over the entire time of occupation it is believed the site was rebuilt, expanded or modified as many as 15 times.

Animals were kept here and there is evidence of weaving and grain storage. To the north a steep down-hill slope would have given the original inhabitants wide views over the surrounding landscape and the chance of spotting early signs of attack.

Below the hill fort, Croft Castle – actually a fortified house – looks out over stunning countryside and the River Lugg. The castle is specially noted for its ornate plaster ceilings. It was heavily remodelled in the 18th century, but its outer appearance suggests 14th- and 15th-century work. There is a lovely walled garden and an avenue of sweet chestnuts.

The castle remained in the Croft family – who had lived here since before the Norman Conquest – until 1746, when it was sold to repay huge debts. Amazingly, a Croft – a descendant of the original family – bought the house back in 1923 and, although now looked after by the National Trust, it is still lived in by members of the family. It's a square house with towers at each corner and there is evidence of work from almost every period, adding greatly to its charm. The nearby medieval church has a magnificent Croft tomb dating from the early 16th century.

Given the beauty and historical significance of the area it seems extraordinary that the place should be such a well-kept secret.

Below: The hill top of Croft Ambrey was inhabited for more than a thousand years, and was built and rebuilt as many as 15 times over that period.

LOWER BROCKHAMPTON

Greenfields, Bringsty, Worcestershire

This late 14th-century manor house is not spectacular – like Hatfield House in Hertfordshire or Audley End in Essex – but in a way this is what makes it so special. It's everything a small English manor house should be: ancient, crooked, mellow and moated, and surrounded by parkland filled with wildlife – from deer and tiny dormice to soaring buzzards – and ancient oak and beech trees; there is a small, timber-framed gatehouse and a ruined chapel. The whole estate is looked after by the National Trust.

The gatehouse is effectively the bridge over the moat. When the house was built – it was probably completed just before 1400 – this area of the Welsh Marches was a dangerous and lawless place. The moat was therefore a genuine defensive feature, as well as, perhaps, a status symbol. The man who had the house built was one John Domulton, a descendant of the Brockhampton family who had lived in this isolated valley since at least the early 12th century.

The house is L-shaped, and has a splendid great hall, open to the rafters. This would have been the venue for varied entertainment, much in the manner of the Saxon halls that would have been found all over England before the Norman Conquest. Huge red-brick chimneys situated at either end of the house seem almost to hold it up, while the gatehouse, with its upper storey jutting precariously out above the lower, looks as if it is about to topple over.

Above: Lower Brockhampton is surely one of the loveliest houses in England, and has changed little since the late 1300s when it was built by John Domulton.

39

Owlpen Manor
Near Uley, Gloucestershire

Owlpen is quintessentially English. This Tudor manor house, which dates back to 1450 and has been little altered since about 1610, sits in a quiet wooded valley in one of the few remaining remote areas of the Cotswolds. It is very difficult to understand how our 18th- and 19th-century forebears could happily demolish hundreds of similar houses on the grounds that they were quaint and old-fashioned, as it is precisely those qualities that we now value so highly.

Owlpen has nothing to do with owls: in Old English the name means 'land enclosed by Olla', presumably a chieftain. By the 12th century the de Olepenne family were living here. In the early 15th century the house and land passed to the Daints, who kept it until the early 20th century. In 1925 the estate was broken up and sold. By sheer good luck, the old manor house – that had been empty for almost a century – was bought and carefully repaired by the arts and crafts architect Norman Jewson.

The manor house, which now houses a collection of arts and crafts furniture, still has its Tudor great hall, a further great chamber with tapestries dating back to 1700 and a beautiful early Georgian parlour. The gardens – there are seven terraces – are filled with old-fashioned roses, box hedges and beautifully clipped yew trees.

Today, Owlpen sits at the centre of a group of historic buildings, including a mill dating from 1728 and a number of cottages, some of which are available for rent as holiday homes. Outside, in every direction, beech woods cover the steep valley sides and miles of woodland paths wander through a landscape rich in flora and fauna.

Left: Tucked away in its own densely wooded valley, Owlpen Manor – the name means 'the land enclosed by Olla' – has changed little since 1610, although much of the fabric of the house dates to about 1450.

DEERHURST

Near Tewkesbury, Gloucestershire

Nowhere in the world is quite like Deerhurst. It is rare to have one Saxon building in a village, but Deerhurst, tucked away in a remote corner of Gloucestershire, boasts two.

The Church of St Mary, with its solid, distinctive tower, looks medieval or perhaps Tudor from the distance, but up close it is quickly apparent from the decorative features that this is a Saxon structure. The farmhouse next to the church and the church itself were originally part of a monastic foundation. The church tower has distinctive herringbone masonry details as well as curious animal-head carvings. The polygonal apse is generally agreed to be 9th-century work.

The first written record of the church dates from 804, in a period known as the Dark Ages because so little evidence of those times survives. Tradition has it that kings from this time were buried here. The earliest, rectangular, part of the building was started in the late 600s, the apse and chapels were added in the 9th century, and the porch was built in the 10th; there are pointed Saxon windows, a small Saxon doorway, and stained glass dating from about 1300.

Just down the road is Deerhurst's other Saxon relic,

again a religious building. Odda's Chapel is now part of a medieval farmhouse. The chapel is tiny, with just two rooms, but still has its original window openings and chancel arch.

An inscribed stone was found nearby in the late 17th century, and states that, 'Earl Odda had this royal hall built and dedicated in honour of the Holy Trinity for the soul of his brother Aelfric'.

Right: The Church of St Mary is one of two Saxon buildings in the tiny Gloucestershire village of Deerhurst. The apse was built in the 800s but the earliest part of the building, the rectangular nave, was probably started in the late 600s.

CLEEVE HILL

Near Cheltenham, Gloucestershire

Cleeve Hill, the highest point in the Cotswolds at 1080 feet (330 metres) above sea level, rises out of a 1000-acre (405-hectare) common. From this wild place you can see far off to the west across the Severn Vale and Malvern Hills, the Forest of Dean and, even further away, to the Black Mountains.

The common still preserves an ancient right that states that 24 local people may graze their animals each summer on the rich limestone grassland. This right dates back more than a thousand years, and was reaffirmed in the 1920s. The common and hill represent a rare survivor of open land from the time before the great Enclosure Acts of the late 18th and early 19th centuries. These acts effectively allowed the rich to remove, without compensation, commoners' rights of access to open land.

Among the increasingly rare plants that thrive on this, the largest area of unspoiled grassland in Gloucestershire, are small scabious and horseshoe vetch, carline thistle and burnet-saxifrage. Butterflies include the beautiful dark green fritillary, and among the more interesting small creatures are the Roman snail (believed to have been eaten by the Romans) and glow-worms.

Below Cleeve Hill there are three stream-filled wooded valleys, quiet and secluded even on the busiest summer day, yet filled with birdsong. Badgers, foxes and deer live undisturbed here.

Below: From Cleeve Hill, the beautiful Cotswold countryside can be seen for miles around. Numerous rare plants and animals thrive in the area, which boasts large tracts of unspoiled grassland.

STANWAY HOUSE

Near Winchcombe, Gloucestershire

Stanway, situated deep in the heart of the Cotswolds and well away from the obvious tourist centres of Broadway and Moreton-in-Marsh, is a remarkable place. The current incumbent is Lord Niedpath, a direct descendant of the Tracy and Charteris branches of the family, who bought the estate in the late 16th century. The previous owners were the abbots of Tewkesbury, who had owned the estate since about 800. Most of the buildings seen today date from 1640–80.

The Jacobean house is built in wonderful yellow Cotswold stone, with a magnificent gatehouse and great hall. The gatehouse – completed in 1630 – is set at right angles to the house. This unusual juxtaposition gives the house a distinctive, almost eccentric, air.

Much of the furniture still used by the family dates back to when the house was first built. There is a curious sprung chair, designed for indoor riding on rainy days, and an enormously long refectory table, made from one huge oak plank, that was almost certainly made specifically for the house. There is also a unique pair of Chippendale day-beds, dating from 1760, and an Elizabethan shuffle board, which is also almost certainly original to the house.

Manorial courts were held in the house until 1800, and even today tenants from the village pay their rents each quarter using a specially built circular table. There is a massive tithe barn, dating from about 1370, which retains its original stone roof and doorway.

The gardens extend to 20 acres (8 hectares), within which are a number of spectacular trees, including cedars of Lebanon, and plans are in hand to restore and reinstate a series of 18th-century waterfalls.

DOVER'S HILL

Near Chipping Campden, Gloucestershire

Named after Robert Dover, the 17th-century historian, this natural amphitheatre looks out over the ancient Cotswold town of Chipping Campden and far beyond to Stratford-upon-Avon and Warwick. In 1612 Dover resurrected the idea of a local Olympic Games and they were held here annually from that year. The games were stopped in 1851, largely because so many competitors were being injured – hardly surprising when you consider that one of the contests was shin kicking!

Below: Once, thousands of English villages had almshouses – evidence of the generosity of long-gone landowners and wealthy merchants who hoped that their concern for the poor would ease their passage into heaven. Few are as unspoiled as these built in Chipping Campden by Sir Baptist Hicks in 1612.

Today, sheep rather than 'athletes' inhabit the hilltop's broad green acres, and it is difficult to believe that the annual Olympics (spelled 'Olympicks' in Dover's day) once attracted crowds in excess of 30,000.

The Dover's Hill Olympics started up again in the late 20th century, but with a little more concern for the health of the competitors – shin kicking is definitely out, for example. But little heed is paid to modern sports: here you will find good old-fashioned tug-of-war competitions, as well as skittles and wrestling.

HICKS'S ALMSHOUSES

Chipping Campden, Gloucestershire

King Harold owned the village and lands of Chipping Campden before the Norman Conquest. Campden

Above: Packwood House is a curious mixture of the fake and the genuine: the house really is Tudor, but, despite appearances, much of the interior is early 20th century.

means 'valley with fields' and Chipping, meaning 'market', also came to be used by the 13th century because a market was held in the town.

Most visitors simply admire the golden stone of the buildings and leave it at that, but Chipping Campden is worth spending some time in as it has some very special buildings indeed.

By the 14th century, the town was remarkably prosperous, its wealth based almost entirely on wool. The Woolstaplers' Hall, an extraordinary survivor in the High Street, dates back to 1340.

Among the wealthy individuals who became rich on the local wool trade was Sir Baptist Hicks. Hicks wanted to do something for the good of the poor – and

the good of his soul – so in 1612 he had a group of almshouses built for 'six poor men and six poor women'. Hicks was one of the richest men in England, but the £1000 he spent on the almshouses was still a staggering sum by the standards of the time. The almshouses continue to be used for their original purpose to this day.

PACKWOOD HOUSE

Lapworth, Warwickshire

This 16th-century house is a fascinating example of the genuine and the fake. The basic house – the walls, floors and ceilings – is certainly Tudor, but the Tudor-style interior was created only in the early 20th century. The endeavour sprang from a general enthusiasm for mock-Tudor in the 1930s, when 'Tudorbethan' housing estates sprang up in suburbs all over the country. At Packwood the mock-Tudor is contained within the genuine article!

There is a large lake in the grounds and a pretty walled garden, as well as famous clipped yews, which stand like Easter Island statues and are said to represent the multitude and the Apostles.

The Featherstone family owned Packwood from the end of the 16th century until 1869, when Alfred Ash bought the house. Mr Ash's son Graham devoted his life to the Tudor refurbishment of the interior and gave the house to the National Trust in 1941.

Another fascinating feature of Packwood House is that it has six sundials – but no one knows why!

SWALCLIFFE BARN
Near Banbury, Oxfordshire

There are just a few surviving examples around the country of those extraordinary cathedral-like barns – tithe barns – that were erected at the end of the Middle Ages to store enough grain for local communities and to collect 'tithes' or taxes. One of the very best is Swalcliffe Barn near Banbury. This great tithe barn was built for New College Oxford by unknown craftsmen of extraordinary skill.

What makes Swalcliffe special is that the vast bulk of its wonderful half-cruck oak roof is intact and substantially unaltered since it was first erected. The barn measures 128 feet (29 metres) long by 23 feet (9.25 metres) wide. The walls are 3 feet (1 metre) thick and nine huge half-cruck timbers support a roof that weighs more than 100 tons.

New College was founded by William of Wykeham and he endowed it with the manor of Swalcliffe, thereby giving the college an income from the land. The decision to build the great barn – recorded in the college records – was taken in 1401 and it took six years to complete an edifice that has now stood unchanged for six centuries.

Today, the barn houses a fascinating collection of historic agricultural vehicles.

GREAT TEW
Near Chipping Norton, Oxfordshire

This lovely village lies on the edge of the north Oxfordshire uplands. Its cottages and houses are made from golden ironstone with thatched or stone roofs and it has the great advantage over some of the more famous Cotswold settlements of looking and feeling like a living village.

At the time of the Domesday Book in 1086, just 53 house-holder tenants were recorded. Over the following centuries, village paths changed, houses collapsed and were rebuilt, but by the 18th century development seems largely to have stopped. In the early 19th century, Matthew Boulton, the Birmingham steam-engine manufacturer, bought the estate – including the village – and made a few alterations. But today the rows of cottages, with their box hedges and backdrop of large ornamental trees, provide a quintessential image of 'olde England', without the 'chocolate-box gloss' typical of so many Cotswold villages.

The secret of the village's 'lived-in' yet timeless appeal is that throughout the 18th and 19th centuries, whenever any of the houses were repaired or even rebuilt, the style that had gone before seems to have been copied. Whatever the latest house-building fashion elsewhere, it was ignored in Great Tew. Even date stones were reinstated in new work, rendering any attempt to accurately date many of the houses all but impossible.

But this is part of the village's enormous charm – this and the fact that there is no modern housing. The pub is truly ancient and the church, which is filled with recently uncovered medieval wall paintings, even more so.

ST OSWALD'S CHURCH
Widford, Oxfordshire

The best way to approach Widford Church is via Burford, a beautiful Cotswold town, with ancient golden stone houses lining its steep main street. Burford is actually just inside Oxfordshire, but is so typical of the Cotswolds at its best that it's hard to believe that it is not officially in Gloucestershire. Half way down the main street, a narrow right turn is signposted to Widford and Swinbrook.

Swinbrook is best known as the childhood home of the celebrated Mitford sisters, the most famous of whom, Nancy (1904–73), was best known for her novel *Love in a Cold Climate*. Well before reaching the village, the sharp-eyed visitor may spot St Oswald's Church in an apparently empty field away to the left. On a slope above the River Windrush sits the small,

Opposite: The cottages of Great Tew epitomize 'olde England': they are steeped in history and whenever rebuilding or repair has been necessary the old styles have been adhered to.

Above: St Oswald's Church is the last remnant of the abandoned medieval village of Widford. The small population that the church once served almost certainly vanished during a devastating outbreak of the Black Death some time in the Middle Ages.

rather lonely looking building.

The single-celled chapel has many ghostly traces of its original wall paintings and is all that remains of the abandoned medieval village of Widford. Traces of the paths and dwellings that stood here before the Black Death devastated the settlement in the Middle Ages are evident from the odd lumps and bumps all over the field surrounding the chapel.

Another fascinating feature is the fact that beneath the church lies a complete mosaic, which is believed to have been part of a Roman villa. The old church flagstones are sometimes lifted in one or two places so visitors can see traces of the mosaic. It's thought that the church builders decided on this site so that they could show physically, as well as metaphorically, how Christianity had supplanted and would forever dominate the old pagan Roman ways.

Widford Church is used occasionally for services and still has its 18th-century box pews.

WAYLAND'S SMITHY

Near Wantage, Oxfordshire

This Neolithic burial chamber sits high up on remote chalk downland on the route of the Ridgeway National Trail. Archaeologists believe that two ditches were originally dug to create a mound, a wooden building was then erected on the mound and at least 14 bodies were placed inside. By the late 4th century BC, the building had gone and the mound had been enlarged to more or less its present size.

Above: The Neolithic burial site known as Wayland's Smithy retains an atmosphere of grandeur, with its massive standing stones and intricate stone interior.

Around 2800 BC, at one end of the mound a cross-shaped stone-lined chamber was created and six standing stones placed at the entrance. Archaeologists believe that at least eight bodies were interred here at that time, but any grave goods that may have accompanied them were stolen long ago. Two of the standing stones are also missing.

There are various theories as to how the tomb acquired its current name. Wayland is believed to have been a Scandinavian god and legend has it that if you leave a coin and your horse at the mound in the evening you will return in the morning to find the horse freshly shod and the coin gone.

The stonework of the tomb lining is of exceptional quality – remarkable when one considers that these stones were placed here so many thousands of years ago.

MAPLEDURHAM HOUSE AND WATERMILL
Mapledurham, Oxfordshire

Situated on the edge of Reading, just half a mile from acres of suburban 1930s semi-detached houses, Mapledurham is an astonishing time capsule. A quiet lane leads from the suburbs to end at the village on the River Thames. An ancient watermill in crumbling mellow red brick still grinds flour on a commercial basis and rows of tiny cottages face across the lane to the big brick mansion that has been occupied by members of the Blount family for more than 500 years.

Mapledurham House was built towards the end of the 16th century, but there had been a substantial timber-framed house on the site for centuries, which passed from the Lyndes family to the Blounts in 1490. Almost a century later, Sir Michael Blount – a lieutenant

at the Tower of London – decided to rebuild, but he had the sense to incorporate parts of the medieval house into his new brick mansion to create what we see today.

The Elizabethan house was again remodelled in the 1820s and given new interiors, but the revamped H-shaped house still retains its tall chimneys, though these have been altered over the years. The plaster ceiling in the great chamber and staircase both date from the 17th century and there is also a great deal of splendid Georgian work. The Blounts were Catholics, and the family's estate was much reduced over the centuries as a result of fines imposed on all those who were not members of the Church of England.

Just alongside Mapledurham House there is a Gothic-revival-style private chapel and the nearby medieval church has a delightful, light-filled interior. The late 15th-century watermill is just a stone's throw away at the side of the Thames.

STONOR PARK

Near Henley-on-Thames, Oxfordshire

The Camoys have lived at Stonor Park for 800 years. Surrounded by the last remnants of what was once a great estate, this ancient house is easy to miss. It lies well off the tourist track that runs along the Thames Valley and concentrates, in this area, on Henley.

Stonor has an extraordinary history. The house has medieval, Tudor and Georgian architectural features, a walled garden, private chapel, and – nearby – an ancient stone circle, evidence that this quiet valley has been inhabited for thousands of years.

When the Camoys arrived in the 13th century, Christianity was still one faith united under the Pope. When Henry VIII decided he wanted a divorce, the Catholic Church and its institutions were systematically destroyed. The Camoys refused to give up the old faith, despite centuries of persecution, which explains the loss of their lands. These were sold off bit by bit to pay fines that were levied on Catholics.

Today, the house still enjoys that remote atmosphere that enabled the Camoys to survive into a new period of toleration. The house has many connections with great figures of the past – the Catholic martyr St Edmund Campion, for example, hid in a concealed room in the attic here. Visitors can see an exhibition of items associated with his life.

The interior of the house now bears the imprint of 18th-century Gothic taste, but the Georgian decoration conceals a far older fabric. The long

gallery has tapestries and family portraits; and there is a magnificent collection of early Italian drawings and fine Georgian and earlier furniture. Perhaps the most unusual thing about Stonor is that mass has been celebrated continuously here in the chapel since 1349, a record unmatched anywhere else in the country.

Opposite: Mapledurham Mill – the last working watermill on the River Thames – is situated on the edge of one of the prettiest villages in the country.

Right: Stonor Park where – uniquely in England – mass has been celebrated continuously since 1349. The house still enjoys a remote atmosphere, despite being just a few miles from the busy town of Henley-on-Thames.

LONDON & THE HOME COUNTIES

London is a fabulously rich place for those keen to seek out little-known houses, museums and monuments. And where fields take over as the Home Counties stretch away from the big city, there's everything from the ancient Hellfire Caves of West Wycombe to the gardens, pubs and hilltops of the Chilterns and North Downs.

KEY

1. Geffrye Museum
2. Kensal Green Cemetery
3. Linley Sambourne House
4. The George Inn
5. London Wetland Centre
6. Cardinal's Wharf
7. Berry Bros & Rudd and Lock & Co. Hatters
8. St Mary's Church
9. Finchampstead Ridges
10. Bekonscot Model Village
11. Hellfire Caves
12. Coombe Hill
13. Waddesdon Manor
14. Claydon House
15. Ivinghoe Beacon
16. Bromham Mill
17. The Swiss Garden
18. Flitton Church and the De Grey Mausoleum
19. Wrest Park
20. Welwyn Roman Baths
21. Shaw's Corner
22. Gardens of the Rose
23. Fighting Cocks

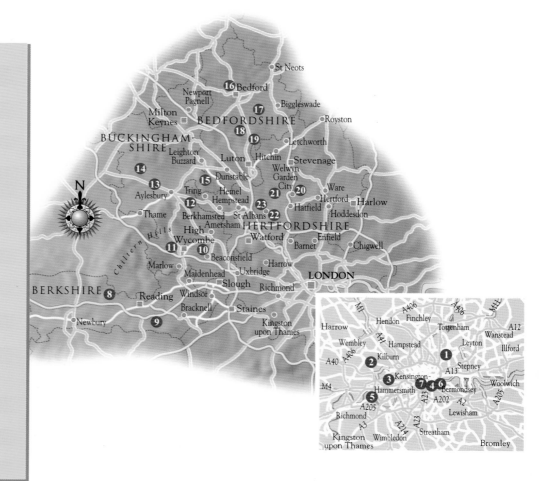

GEFFRYE MUSEUM
Shoreditch, London

With its jaded air of derelict commercial prosperity, Kingsland Road in London's East End is an unlikely setting for a row of exquisite 18th-century almshouses. The Geffrye almshouses, built by Sir Robert Geffrye for the Ironmongers' Company in 1715, now house one of the most interesting exhibitions in the country.

Here, well away from the main tourist areas of the capital city, you will find a remarkable collection of English furniture, pictures and other fittings in a series of chronologically arranged period rooms.

This is like time travel on foot, as a tour of the museum leads visitors through typical rooms from the early 17th century to the present day. There is the dark, beautiful, early oak furniture and panelling of the Elizabethans, the light and elegance of Georgian drawing rooms, heavy Victorian interiors and rooms filled with utility furniture and early televisions from the 1950s.

The best thing about the museum, however, is that the interiors reflect in many instances the life of the less well-off and the attention to detail is remarkable.

KENSAL GREEN CEMETERY
North Kensington, London

Most visitors brave enough to include a cemetery on their London itinerary go to Highgate Cemetery in the north of the city. But tucked away by the side of the Grand Union Canal over to the west in what was – until recently – a fairly poor part of North Kensington, is Kensal Green Cemetery, an extraordinary monument to Victorian funeral piety.

Until the coming of the canal in the 18th century this was a quiet place: there were a few houses at the

Below: This fabulous Georgian interior at the Geffrye Museum is just one exhibit in a museum dedicated to recreating typical rooms from the past.

Above: An elaborate tomb in Kensal Green Cemetery where the quiet leafy paths and walks are filled with wildlife and birdsong.

junction of Harrow Road and Kilburn Lane, but the rest of the area was open farmland, with the odd isolated inn, a day's walk from London.

By the early 1800s, however, the small village, centred round the junction and its green, was expanding and by the 1830s London's church graveyards were filled to bursting. In 1832 All Souls Cemetery, as Kensal Green Cemetery was originally known thanks to the land being owned by All Souls College Oxford, was opened to ease the problem of graveyard overcrowding.

Within a few years Kensal Green Cemetery – as it quickly became known – was the fashionable place to be buried. Among the cemetery's many extraordinary monuments are Greek temples, miniature Egyptian halls and medieval castles, Gothic fantasies, as well as more ordinary but equally fascinating gravestones and tombs. Look out for the final resting place of Sir Anthony Panizzi (1797–1879), who created the famous round reading room at the British Library (now part of the British Museum); Charles Babbage (1791–1871), who developed the first computer; authors Wilkie Collins (1824–89), William Makepeace Thackeray (1811–63) and Anthony Trollope (1815–82);

as well as the greatest of all the Victorian engineers, Isambard Kingdom Brunel (1806–59).

The cemetery is full of mature trees and shrubs and gives every indication of being deep in the heart of the countryside: narrow paths meander through the thick undergrowth and the roar of traffic stills to quiet. This is one of London's best and richest wildlife sites, with dozens of bird species, squirrels and foxes, butterflies and moths.

LINLEY SAMBOURNE HOUSE
Kensington, London

What an extraordinary place this is. Great houses and churches often survive intact, but the interiors of the houses of the middle and working classes tend to vanish without trace. Linley Sambourne House is an exception.

Named after the cartoonist who lived here from 1874 to 1910, this is a perfect example of a well-to-do but by no means aristocratic household of the mid-Victorian period. When Sambourne and his young wife moved into the house, which had been built only four years earlier, they decorated it in the then fashionable aesthetic style, characterized by heavy velvet drapes,

William Morris wallpapers, ornate Turkish carpets and a vast clutter of china ornaments.

Sambourne earned his living as a cartoonist, mostly for the satirical magazine *Punch*, for almost half a century. Most of his drawings were created in this house and numerous examples of his work are on display, along with his photographs: like many artists of the time he was fascinated by this still relatively new art form.

By sheer luck, the house remained substantially unchanged through the 20th century. The Sambournes' son, Roy, inherited the house and did little to it, probably because he never married. When he died he left it to his elder sister, Maud. She too was passionate about preserving it intact, largely because – as she said herself – she'd been so happy there as a child. Her daughter Anne then used the house. At a party in 1957, Anne proposed that she and her friends, who included the Poet Laureate Sir John Betjeman, should found a Victorian Society to preserve the house and its contents. The society would also work for the preservation of other similar examples of Victorian taste – the Victorian style was then hugely unpopular.

Tours of the house are by arrangement.

Below: The George Inn is a unique relic of the stagecoach era, when similar hostelries would have been regularly found along Britain's various stagecoach routes.

THE GEORGE INN
Southwark, London

The George Inn is London's last surviving example of a style of building that was common throughout the long centuries when all transport was by horse. There has been an inn on the site of The George since the 14th century, but the present building dates from just after a huge fire in 1676, which destroyed most of Southwark.

Around that period there were at least half a dozen galleried inns in London, built round a courtyard, with the rooms on each level leading onto a walkway or gallery. This style of building would have been familiar to Shakespeare and his contemporaries. Photographs exist of at least two of London's lost galleried inns and show that the style of these buildings was remarkably similar to that of The George Inn.

The courtyard enabled coaches to enter and be unloaded in the middle of the building. On the ground floor would have been public rooms for drinking and eating, with bedrooms entered via the external galleries above. The George retains this arrangement and though you can no longer stay at the inn you may still drink in the bars.

The oldest of The George's bars still has its 18th-century interior, with tavern clock, crooked timber

floors, two fireplaces and benches built into the walls. It is without question a Southwark scene from at least two centuries ago. Sadly this small 'tap room', as it is known, has not been used as a bar since the 1980s, but it can still be visited. Only one side of what would have originally been a four-sided inn still exists, but when you look up from the courtyard towards the galleries above you will experience an authentic view of London past. The novelist Charles Dickens (1812–70) mentions The George by name in *Little Dorrit*.

Throughout the coaching era, The George was the starting point for thousands of huge wagons leaving London each week for Sussex, Kent and Surrey. Stagecoaches carrying passengers ran almost continually day and night, and the inn would have been the scene of constant activity. The arrival of the railways in the early 19th century put paid to the coaching inns, but The George survived into the 20th century by using its yard for a hop market. The railway company that owned it nearly caused its demolition in the 1930s, but fortunately decided at the last minute to give what remained to the National Trust.

Below: The London Wetland Centre has all the atmosphere of some distant fenland landscape, with its marshes and thousands of resident waterbirds and waders.

LONDON WETLAND CENTRE
Barnes, London

There is nothing quite like this anywhere else in the world. In the heart of one of the biggest cities on earth is a wildlife reserve of more than 105 acres (42.5 hectares). The mixture of habitats was created from disused waterworks – the reservoirs here once supplied Londoners with clean water, until demand outstripped supply and new, larger reservoirs were built further from the metropolis – and include grassland, mudflats, reed beds and open lakes.

Paths lead through and around this wild and very natural-looking place, which attracts a host of rare and not-so-rare species of duck, geese and waders. There are hides, and visitors are presented with binoculars for the duration of their tour. Depending on the time of year, you might see grebe, cormorant, heron, kingfisher, tern, widgeon, mallard, coot and tufted duck. There are more than 30 ponds and lakes, nearly 3 miles (5km) of walkways, 27,000 trees and more than 200,000 aquatic plants.

Children are given little nets and allowed to fish for larvae and water insects, and there is always a member of staff on hand to help out.

CARDINAL'S WHARF

Bankside, London

This is a tall, narrow house – once part of a terrace – which overlooks the Thames on the south bank of the river opposite St Paul's Cathedral. It is the earliest and sole surviving example of the many Bankside houses that once lined the river, near to the spot where William Shakespeare's plays were first performed.

When Henry VIII's wife Catherine of Aragon arrived from Spain in the early 16th century she stayed here. Almost two centuries later, when Christopher Wren was building St Paul's, he too stayed in the house to supervise the work on his great cathedral.

Although it has been altered over the years, the house is basically 16th-century. It stands almost next door to the recreated Globe Theatre and running down one side – sadly now closed to the public – can be found one of London's narrowest thoroughfares – Cardinal Cap Alley. The house is privately owned.

BERRY BROS & RUDD AND LOCK & CO. HATTERS

St James's, London

St James's Street, that elegant sloping thoroughfare leading from Piccadilly down to the Tudor gateway of St James's Palace, was once lined with humble shops, before the rich built their grand houses and clubs in the 18th century. Two of these shops, by some small miracle, remain.

Wine merchants Berry Bros & Rudd began trading here at the end of the 17th century and when you step inside it is obvious that very little has changed

Right: The little house at Cardinal's Wharf is a lonely relic of the rows of tall narrow houses that occupied much of the river-front in Elizabethan times.

in terms of decoration, fixtures and fittings in the intervening 300 years. Ancient floors and benches slope in all directions and the walls are crooked, as befits a property that is even older than it looks.

Lord Byron bought his wine here, as did the Duke of Wellington, the actor Laurence Olivier and the novelist Evelyn Waugh. The business is still family-owned and run. Next to the shop, an ancient, narrow lane leads to a tiny secluded courtyard, a quaint reminder of the dense network of tiny lanes and courts that once characterized London.

City of London. The bowler actually started life as a gamekeeper's hat. It was designed for the immensely wealthy Lord Coke of Norfolk, whose gamekeepers were occasionally attacked by poachers: the bowler was an early form of crash helmet! How it made the transition to the Square Mile is something of a mystery. But Lock's reputation has spread far and wide. The company was even mentioned in Sir John Betjeman's great autobiographical poem *Summoned by Bells*.

St Mary's Church
Aldworth, Berkshire

The church of St Mary's in this hilltop village on the Berkshire Downs hides an extraordinary secret – the so-called Aldworth Giants. Hidden away inside a church that you might easily pass by without a second thought is the most magnificent set of 14th-century monuments in Britain. The 'giants' are in fact effigies, and were placed here for the de la Beche family, probably in the 1340s. They were almost certainly commissioned by Nicholas de la Beche, who lived at La Beche Castle, which has long since vanished.

The nine reclining effigies (which were badly damaged during the English Civil War) dominate the church. One of the figures is so tall that he can't lie flat, but is propped on one elbow. Two male figures lie under the arches of the south wall; between them is a figure believed to be Joan, wife of Sir Nicholas. Sir Nicholas himself lies in the middle of the church with his head resting on a shield, wearing a helmet. Sir John and Isabelle de la Beche lie at the entrance to the chancel, and against the north wall is another John, as well as Sir Robert and the oversized giant figure of Philip de la Beche.

Outside is an ancient yew that was probably planted in the 12th century, about the time the church was built.

Lock & Co. Hatters, just a few doors down from Berry Bros, has been making hats in London since the 17th century. Since 1764, the business has been run from this shop. Its interiors and fixtures have changed little: creaking timber shelves hold hats of all kinds, and an extraordinary device – a conformator – is still used to measure each client's head. The details, including distinguishing lumps and bumps, are then kept on file so that new hats can be made to order, even if the customer is on the other side of the world.

Locks have made hats for everyone from Admiral Lord Nelson to Charlie Chaplin. Most famously they invented the bowler hat, which was, until the 1960s, the universal headgear of male office workers in the

Above: Based in one of London's oldest and quirkiest shops, Lock & Co. Hatters have been making headwear for the gentry of London since the 17th century.

Right: Finchampstead Ridges, a beautiful and little-known ridge of ancient pines above the Blackwater Valley.

FINCHAMPSTEAD RIDGES
Finchampstead, Berkshire

The National Trust's Finchampstead Ridges deserve to be better known. Ancient pines and heather typify the ridges, which seem almost to float above the south-facing slopes of the Blackwater Valley.

The National Trust also owns Simon's Wood, on the northern slope of the valley. Hereabouts there are rare remnants of ancient heathland, which provide suitable habitats for numerous, sometimes rare, plants and animals: here you may see siskin and spotted flycatcher, as well as woodlark, robin and blackbird. Rare plants include purple moor grass and marsh pennywort.

Paths weave in and out of this beautiful yet little-visited valley. At the bottom of the valley slope is Spout Pond, a refuge for once numerous but now threatened species of common frog and toad. The pond also provides a home for numerous gorgeously coloured species of damselfly and dragonfly.

BEKONSCOT MODEL VILLAGE
Beaconsfield, Buckinghamshire

The British seem to love life in miniature. How many fathers have bought their children train sets only to find that they themselves spend far more time playing with the trains than their offspring? Then there's miniature golf and, most curious of all, miniature villages.

Among the most extraordinary of these scaled-down worlds is Bekonscot Model Village. The village – the oldest of its type in the world – was the brainchild of accountant Roland Callingham. Callingham began work on his Lilliputian creation in a field in Beaconsfield in the 1920s. He built miniature houses in the style of the time and dug a pretend village pond. He then joined forces with his friend James

Below: Roland Callingham created Bekonscot in the Buckinghamshire countryside in 1929. The miniature village reflects English life as it was between the wars.

Shilcock whose passion was miniature railways. Soon Bekonscot's rate of growth was matching that of the nearby garden cities of Letchworth and Welwyn.

From the day the village opened to the public in 1929, the emphasis has been on raising money for charity – indeed, more than £1 million has been distributed among various charities in the 70-plus years that Bekonscot has existed.

After some attempts in the 1980s to bring the village up to date – housing estates and shopping centres were built – it was decided that it would have more appeal if it reflected the style of living and architecture of the 1930s, which is precisely what it now does: steam trains chug round the site, passing miniature windmills, and a brass band plays merrily on the end of the pier.

Below: The Hellfire Caves were said to be the haunt of atheists and devil worshippers in the 18th century, but the area was almost certainly mined in prehistoric times for flint.

The miniature train now links six miniature villages, each with its own character and miniature population. Village entertainments of an earlier time are also represented: there's a fair, a zoo and a cricket match. A gauge one railway – that's a model railway big enough to carry real passengers – has been added so visitors can now enjoy the model world from the comfort of their steam-train seats.

HELLFIRE CAVES
West Wycombe, Buckinghamshire

The aristocrat Sir Francis Dashwood and a number of his friends set up what was known as the Hellfire Club some time in the mid-18th century. Other Hellfire Clubs existed, but this was the best known because its members were so well bred. Dashwood's gang had originally been known as the Monks of Medmenham because they met at Medmenham Abbey on the Thames, but when this was destroyed by fire they had to find a new home. From that time on, the club met in the old chalk mines to the west of West Wycombe.

The club is reputed to have been involved in all sorts of devilish activities, including orgies and lengthy drinking bouts. Worst of all – from the authorities' point of view – the club was a haven for freemasonry and free thinking, and the secluded caves provided the ideal meeting place.

The caves are flint-rich and were almost certainly mined in prehistoric times. Sir Francis had them enlarged in the late 1740s to provide work for local unemployed men and to make them usable for the club's meetings. The caves extend up to 300 feet (98 metres) below ground.

Young aristocratic tearaways had been a feature of English life since the Middle Ages, and they had flourished under Charles II's reign. Dashwood's cohorts echoed the activities of the Earl of Rochester and the Duke of Buckingham, rakes of the Restoration court who could say and do as they liked under the king's protection.

The 11th Baronet – a direct descendant of Sir Francis Dashwood – restored the caves in the 1950s. Today they are pretty much as they were in Dashwood's time, with the modern addition of life-sized waxwork figures in 18th-century costume. Walking through the passageways and huge banqueting hall, it is extraordinary to think that they were all dug by hand.

COOMBE HILL

Wendover, Buckinghamshire

Coombe Hill, the highest point in the Chilterns, is a spectacular hilltop within easy reach of London. It's the sort of place you would expect to find in a more remote rural location, rather than on the edge of one of the world's great conurbations. From the top, the Aylesbury Valley and the long ridge of the Chilterns can be seen stretching away for miles and woodland paths wind across the huge acreage, owned by the National

Above: A monument to the dead of the Boer Wars (1881 and 1899–1902) tops Coombe Hill, the highest point on the Chilterns.

Trust, through quiet glades and across open ground.

Sheep have been introduced to control invasive scrub species, so this chalky downland looks much as it would have done in the 18th and preceding centuries when sheep were the mainstay of the economy. The rich grassland environment is home to myriad species – harebell, wild thyme, vetch, wild strawberry and rock-rose, among others. On the flatter areas there are oak and beech trees and there is evidence of ancient coppice in the nearby Low Scrubs area of wooded common. This was once common land where poor villagers could gather firewood.

On the summit of Coombe Hill is a monument to a conflict now largely forgotten – the Boer Wars. Erected in 1904, the elegant obelisk was destroyed by lightning in the 1930s before being restored. It had to be concealed during the Second World War (1939–45) to prevent it being used as a marker by enemy aircraft.

WADDESDON MANOR

Waddesdon, Buckinghamshire

Built in the French Renaissance style between 1874 and 1889, this National Trust property is a fake château nestling in the Buckinghamshire countryside. The interior is fabulous. Waddesdon was built for a family that was, and still is, one of the richest in the world: the Rothschilds.

Baron Ferdinand de Rothschild, who commissioned the house, was a passionate Francophile – hence the extraordinary exterior – who filled Waddesdon with magnificent works of art and pictures.

The priceless collection includes Sèvres porcelain, Savonnerie carpets, Beauvais tapestries and furniture made for the French royal family. English works of art include pieces by Gainsborough and Reynolds. There are also masterpieces by 17th-century Flemish and Dutch painters, as well as a superb collection of arms and armour.

The Victorian gardens are equally impressive, with superb displays of bedding plants, a parterre, a knot garden and numerous exotic trees.

CLAYDON HOUSE

Middle Claydon, Buckinghamshire

Claydon House is by no means among the best known of the National Trust's properties. It was never a great palace like Blenheim or Hatfield, but its interior is uniquely beautiful and extraordinary.

The second Lord Verney built the house in 1768, but this was really a recreation of a much earlier house. A huge west wing was added, though never completed. What remains today is just one section of the original house, and its rooms are decorated in a style that portrays the first flowering of a passion for all things oriental. The main motifs are pagodas, oriental birds and exquisite summer houses, and the decoration includes some of the best woodcarving in Europe. The 18th-century craftsman responsible for the work was Luke Lightfoot, whose intricate figures will stand comparison

Left: The château style of Waddesdon Manor reflects its first owner's passion for France. The house was built by the fabulously wealthy Rothschilds.

with almost anything by the great Grinling Gibbons.

Florence Nightingale (1820–1910) – a relative of the Verney family – was a frequent visitor, and mementos of her life can be seen in the room in which she slept.

Claydon is set in its own park, which sweeps down to three beautiful lakes, the home of giant bronze-coloured carp and dangerous pike. The house is said to be haunted.

IVINGHOE BEACON
Chiltern Hills, Buckinghamshire

Like Coombe Hill, Ivinghoe Beacon is another hilltop with breathtaking views, relatively close to London. With its Iron Age hill fort, Ivinghoe is actually part of one of the National Trust's biggest estates, Ashridge, which runs right along the Chiltern Hills through Hertfordshire and Buckinghamshire. The estate is an impressive mixture of heathland, downland, ancient woodland, common and open hilltop. Much of it is a designated Site of Special Scientific Interest.

The downland was once grazed by sheep, giving it a distinctive cropped look, but due to economic reasons the sheep largely vanished in the 1930s and have only been reintroduced recently by the National Trust in an effort to restore the spectacular hilltop to its earlier state. There are also ancient pollarded trees in the little hamlet of Frithsden, and sunken droveways below the beacon.

The estate woodland, heath and common are home to many rare species of plant and animal, including sparrowhawk, woodcock, firecrest and tawny owl. On the slopes below the beacon you might be lucky enough to see a Duke of Burgundy fritillary butterfly.

Below: Looking towards the Iron Age hill fort at Ivinghoe Beacon, the landscape is a wonderful mix of heathland, downland and ancient woodland.

BROMHAM MILL

Bromham, Bedfordshire

Corn has been ground at Bromham Mill on the River Ouse for centuries. Set in almost 7 acres (3 hectares) of watermeadows, near the remarkable Georgian 26-arch Bromham Bridge, the mill provides a glorious glimpse of how England used to be.

There has been a mill here since Saxon times, but the current picturesque building dates from the end of the 17th century, with Georgian and Victorian additions. It's a lovely mix of stonework, old brick and timber framing.

Originally there were two undershot wheels, but an iron breastwheel (installed in 1908) now provides the power for the wooden cogs and wheels. Watching this example of early technology in action is quite fascinating: the notches on the great wheel all had to be cut and fitted by hand; the mechanism is an extraordinary monument to the skills of long-dead craftsmen.

The mill and the buildings nearby – blacksmith's shop, piggery and several cottages – was once a self-sufficient community. A great eel trap by the water-wheel is recorded as having once taken more than a hundredweight of eels in one night and an apple orchard provided both food and the right kind of timber for the gear teeth on the mill-wheels.

THE SWISS GARDEN

Old Warden, Bedfordshire

The Swiss Garden, with its wandering peacocks and curiously alpine feel, really does deserve to be appreciated by a wider audience. Its 10 acres (4 hectares) are home to a mix of flowers, rare trees and garden architecture that reflect the fashion of the 1820s when the craze for all things Swiss was at its height.

Rare trees and shrubs surround a maze of wandering paths that either circle ponds or cross them via elaborate wrought-iron bridges. In the centre of the garden is the little thatched Swiss cottage from which this delightful place gets its name. In addition to the cottage there is what our ancestors would probably have called a ferny grotto – a sort of dark cave that is lit occasionally by shafts of light from outside and which is very mysterious in a slightly contrived way.

Left: Flour is now ground at Bromham Mill to inform today's generation of how the local natural resources were harnessed for power.

Opposite: The magnificent marble De Grey monuments, all of which are exceedingly naturalistic, lie in a church that has all the appearance of a castle. The earliest monument was completed in 1545.

The Swiss Garden was the creation of Lord Ongley, and is the best example we still have of the early 19th-century idea of a typical Swiss garden. The architect of the garden buildings was probably John Buonarotti Papworth, who suggested that bark should be used as cladding to give that genuine rustic look!

FLITTON CHURCH AND THE DE GREY MAUSOLEUM

Flitton, Bedfordshire

It is curious how small, apparently ordinary churches sometimes conceal remarkable architectural gems. Flitton's church, dedicated to St John the Baptist, is a case in point. With its three-stage tower and castellations – which continue right round the building – 15th-century Flitton Church, built in richly coloured local sandstone, has the look of a squat castle. Adjoining the church is the 17th-century white stucco De Grey Mausoleum, a chancel filled with the monuments of one family.

The earliest of these is to Sir Henry de Grey, Earl of Kent, who died in 1545. All the monuments – and they continued to be made into Victorian times – are detailed and naturalistic, and no expense seems to have been spared in the use of marble. They include the ninth earl (died 1651) and his wife Anabella, who died in 1658. A later Henry, who died in 1748, is portrayed in Roman dress.

The de Grey family lived at nearby Wrest Park, and their devotion to the family mausoleum is unmatched elsewhere. The church is also notable as the last resting place of one Thomas Hill, who died, we are assured, in 1601 at the grand old age of 128!

WREST PARK

Silsoe, Bedfordshire

The earls of Kent – the de Grey family – lived at Wrest Park for nearly 600 years. In that time, they built three houses on the same site, and the last – a French-

Above: Welwyn Roman Baths lie hidden, but still accessible to those in the know, beneath the main A1(M) road. The baths are over 1750 years old.

mythological figures, coats-of-arms and monumental classical pillars, this is the only example of Hauduroy's work on public view in England.

The domed pleasure pavilion, one of the finest buildings in Wrest Park's landscape, was designed by Thomas Archer (*c.* 1668–1743), who was much influenced by his lengthy travels through Europe. Today, however, he is far less well known than his contemporaries, such as Nicholas Hawksmoor (1661–1736).

Elsewhere, a beautiful canal crosses the gardens and mature avenues of trees planted by Capability Brown in *c.* 1758 still survive. There is a bath-house with white marble fountains, classical ruins and an orangery.

WELWYN ROMAN BATHS
Welwyn, Hertfordshire

Road builders usually destroy everything in their path, but not always – which is why drivers on the A1(M) in Hertfordshire now roar above one of the county's best-kept secrets. Beneath the busy modern roadway, engineers managed to preserve in situ a remarkable Roman bath-house, which was once part of a much larger villa complex.

Evidence of the Romans' ingenious underfloor heating system survives here, together with the various rooms that provided water for both hot and tepid baths and freezing plunge pools. You can still see where slaves, who had to work continuously to stoke the fires that heated the floors and water, would have sat.

There are numerous displays showing how Roman life in the area was organized and visitors can walk from bath to bath, just as the Romans did all those years ago.

style château built in 1834 – still stands. It is now home to the National Institute of Agricultural Engineering, but English Heritage allows visitors in to see the state rooms.

The 90-acre (36.5-hectare) garden and the pavilion are the real hidden treasures here. The Baroque pavilion has a magnificent set of early 18th-century *trompe-l'oeil* wall paintings by the French artist Louis Hauduroy. Completed in 1712, and featuring

SHAW'S CORNER

Near Welwyn, Hertfordshire

The great playwright George Bernard Shaw (1856–1950) refused ever to romanticize the past; he believed in the future and in the power of science and technology to transform our lives – which may explain why he refused to buy the sort of picturesque 'olde worlde' country mansion so beloved of the newly wealthy British. Instead he bought himself a contemporary, functional house. Today Shaw's Corner, an Edwardian villa built in 1902, looks anything but contemporary, but it does capture perfectly the spirit of Edwardian times and of the man who lived here with his wife Charlotte from 1906 until his death in 1950.

The house is red brick, solid and unremarkable, except for some lovely Arts and Crafts brick details. It was originally built as the rectory for the little village of Eyot St Lawrence, but what makes it fascinating today is that all the rooms are much as Shaw left them, with furniture and personal possessions in their places, as if the playwright and his wife had just gone out for a walk.

Below: The great early 20th-century playwright George Bernard Shaw (1856–1950) lived in this quiet corner of Hertfordshire for more than 40 years. The summer house has been left exactly as it was in Shaw's lifetime.

The summer house, well away from the main house at the bottom of the garden, looks as it would have done when Shaw arrived each morning to begin work. It was built especially so it could be turned to follow the sun as it moved round the house.

Shaw's star has waned in recent years as the brand of optimism to which he subscribed in plays such as *Man and Superman* has come to seem naïve, but between 1920 and 1950 he was probably the world's most famous playwright and his opinions were sought on a thousand subjects that had nothing to do with his plays.

Despite the long years that he lived here, Shaw claimed he never liked the house. However, he loved the garden and he once said that gardening was one of the few useful things a man could do in life; he was clipping his roses on the day he died.

The garden extends to more than 3.5 acres (1.4

hectares) and Shaw walked it with his wife each day when the weather was fine. When they had covered a mile, Shaw would place a pebble on the ground to mark the spot.

GARDENS OF THE ROSE
St Albans, Hertfordshire

Tucked away in this pretty corner of Hertfordshire is the most extraordinary collection of roses. Here, among 30,000 different varieties, you will find the old and the new, the rare and the common.

Run by the Royal National Rose Society, the gardens demonstrate the English passion for this ubiquitous flower. There are also displays of what are known as 'companion plants', that is, those other species that co-exist happily with roses.

There are vast beds of roses everywhere: climbers, standards, dwarf varieties and much more. Here you will find everything from Seagull to Bobby James, from

Below: More than 30,000 varieties of Britain's favourite flower, including hybrids, climbers, shrubs and old tea roses, can be found in the Gardens of the Rose in St Albans.

Summer Wine to Kiftsgate. There are broad terraces, small formal gardens and arbours. All in all, there really is nothing quite like it anywhere else for the rose lover. The Queen Mother Garden includes a huge selection of old-fashioned roses and there are trial grounds and a peace garden, too.

Over a hundred varieties of clematis are also on view and judicious planting means that something spectacular will be blooming all season.

FIGHTING COCKS
St Albans, Hertfordshire

Several pubs have laid claim to being the oldest in the country, but a strong contender for the title – and one that is currently accepted by the *Guinness Book of Records* – is the Fighting Cocks in the heart of old St Albans.

The pub sits below the great cathedral, which tends to be the main draw for visitors to the town. As a result, the Fighting Cocks is easily missed. Parts of this picturesque crooked timber building are certainly extraordinarily old: elements dating back to the mid-11th century and pretty much every period since have been identified.

The exact history of the Fighting Cocks is difficult to trace. This 11th-century structure is built on an 8th-century site, but has probably not always been an inn. There is evidence – hotly disputed by some – that the Fighting Cocks was a pigeon house before it became an alehouse in 1485.

Whatever the rights and wrongs of the argument, the Fighting Cocks is undoubtedly very old indeed and one of its bars was formerly a cock-fighting pit. It

Above: The Fighting Cocks in St Albans is officially Britain's oldest pub; there is some evidence that it was also used as a pigeon house in medieval times.

is also said that Oliver Cromwell (1599–1658), who stayed here on one his many forays into the English countryside to muster troops against the Royalist army, insisted on keeping his horse in the bar while he slept upstairs.

SURREY, SUSSEX & KENT

The south-east has probably been inhabited for longer than any other region of England and, despite new roads and urban development, it has rural areas that appear entirely untouched by the modern world.

KEY

1. Chatley Heath Semaphore Tower
2. Headley Common
3. Chaldon Church
4. Holmbury Hill
5. Leith Hill
6. Parham House and Gardens
7. St Botolph's Church
8. Cissbury Ring
9. Chyngton Farm
10. Jack Fuller's Pyramid
11. Bateman's
12. The Mermaid Inn
13. St Augustine's Church
14. Derek Jarman's Garden
15. St Leonard's Church
16. The Grand Shaft

CHATLEY HEATH SEMAPHORE TOWER
Chatley Heath, Surrey

Rapid communications systems are not entirely the preserve of the modern world – which is precisely why the Chatley Heath Semaphore Tower is so interesting. And quite apart from the fascinating exhibitions on early naval communication that occupy the tower, there are 700 acres (283.5 hectares) of beautiful grounds, offering glorious views north to London and across the North Downs.

The 60-foot-high (18-metre) semaphore tower was built in 1822, and was just one of a chain of towers built by the Navy to link the Admiralty in London to the fleet at Portsmouth. As the signal on the top of each tower could instantly be seen by the signal recorder at the next, who then passed it on, communication would have been extraordinarily fast, even by today's standards.

Today, visitors can stand on the platform where the tower superintendent would have stood, telescope in hand, to spot the last signal, and you can even see how the semaphore mast was originally used.

Right: Chatley Heath Semaphore Tower is one of England's last surviving buildings associated with an early form of information technology.

HEADLEY COMMON
Near Dorking, Surrey

Although commons are a relatively rare habitat today, before the great period of enclosure at the end of the 18th century much of Britain was unfenced common land. By ancient tradition, such land was available to

71

villagers to graze their animals, to gather bedding for both animals and humans and to gather firewood. The great lords who owned the huge estates passed legislation to take the commons from the ordinary villagers, and tens of thousands of acres vanished into private ownership. However, one or two remnants of what was once a widespread system of land management do remain, and one of the very best is Headley Common, near well-known Box Hill.

Over 500 acres (202 hectares) – the biggest remaining area of heathland on the North Downs – were acquired by the National Trust in 1946 from the Lord of the Manor, who had allowed local people to continue to exercise their ancient grazing rights. The land had never been ploughed, but bracken and scrub had encroached on what was once open grazing country. It was only after a lengthy period of restoration by the Trust that Headley Common regained its earlier appearance. A key element of the Trust's restoration project was the introduction of Highland cattle.

Below: The great medieval wall painting at Chaldon has all the look and feel of the Middle Ages, when every church in the country would have been similarly painted.

As you admire the views and enjoy the walks at this lovely spot, often ignored by those who head straight for Box Hill, you may also come across rare species such as slow worms, great crested newts, linnets and woodlarks. The ponds on the common are home to lavishly coloured dragonflies and delicate damselflies.

CHALDON CHURCH
Chaldon, Surrey

Many ancient churches have something of an over-restored look about them, but Chaldon is different: it has the appearance and feel of the Dark Ages, largely because of the size and condition of the magnificent 17-foot (5.2-metre) medieval mural on its west wall.

A church was recorded here in the 8th-century Charter of Frithwald, but the present building dates mostly from the mid-12th century. Originally just a simple rectangular nave, it has been extended over the centuries, but still reflects the aspirations of what would have been a humble community, far from the centres of wealth and power.

Above: Holmbury Hill overlooks the Weald, which means wilderness or forest, and its dense woodlands. This is a landscape that has changed little over the last five centuries.

The mural covers the whole of the west wall and, despite centuries of being hidden beneath ever-deepening layers of whitewash, it survives in superlative condition. It is a Day of Judgement and Ladder of Salvation scene, showing white figures on an eerie ochre-coloured background. We witness how the righteous are saved and the damned are sent to hell for eternity. If our medieval ancestors believed such scenes existed in the afterlife, then it is no wonder they flocked regularly to church.

When one considers that 98 per cent of all medieval religious art was destroyed during the Reformation – and almost all medieval English art was religious – the survival of this large mural is all the more miraculous. It was discovered under layers of paint during restoration work in the 1860s and justifies entirely the church's Grade 1 listing.

HOLMBURY HILL
Near Holmbury St Mary, Surrey

Holmbury Hill is part of the three-hill chain – Holmbury, Leith and Pitch – that overlooks miles of wooded countryside in the Weald. It is a place that gives the lie to the idea that Surrey is made up entirely of stockbroker-belt housing and arterial roads, for this is remarkably wild country.

The countryside hereabouts is rich in woodland plants and animals, as well as heathland birds and even rare snakes. At the top of the hill you can enjoy breathtaking views and the sight of an occasional kestrel hovering overhead.

Holmbury Hill is cared for by Hurtwood Control, a unique organization whose purpose is to keep this privately owned countryside open to the public. The wooded slopes are criss-crossed by footpaths and bridleways and there is a fantastic sense of history here. The pattern of ancient settlement can still be seen – hill

Above: Leith Hill's folly tower arguably turned a big hill into a mountain by pushing it over the magic 1000-foot (305-metre) mark.

LEITH HILL
Near Coldharbour, Surrey

Leith Hill, which at 965 feet (294 metres) is the highest point in the south-east of England, falls just 35 feet (11 metres) short of being classified as a mountain.

It's a lovely and spectacular spot that also has a colourful history. In 1765 the then owner, Richard Hull, decided that he would break the magic 1000-foot (305-metre) barrier by hook or by crook, so he added a folly tower (taking the hill to 1069 feet/325 metres) from which he and his friends could look out across 13 counties. Visitors can still take in the views from the tower today.

Less well known than the tower is the beautiful surrounding land: the ancient wooded slopes and nearby heathland of Dukes Warren and Coldharbour Common are rich in wildlife, tranquil walks and rare plants and flowers.

This whole area is an astonishing haven of peace and quiet. The oak and hazel woods at Leith Hill are filled with bluebells in spring and rhododendrons in May and June, as well as rare woodland herbs, such as sweet woodruff and yellow archangel. Butterflies include the rare white admiral, and tree-creepers, nuthatches and wood warblers, among other birds, can be found.

fort remnants on the hilltops, medieval villages in the valleys and isolated farms and country houses.

The Surrey Hills, though now often overshadowed by the more spectacular landscapes of the Lake District and elsewhere, were once the inspiration for artists and poets. In the 18th and 19th centuries, landscape painters flocked to the three hills, together with poets such as John Keats (1795–1821) and Alfred, Lord Tennyson (1809–92), the diarist John Evelyn (1620–1706) and the composer Ralph Vaughan Williams (1872–1958).

PARHAM HOUSE AND GARDENS
Near Pulborough, West Sussex

This beautiful Elizabethan manor house is less well known than many similar houses because it has never been taken into public ownership. Three families have owned Parham since building began in 1577: the Palmers, the Bishops and the Pearsons.

Little has been changed or damaged over the years and the many-gabled stone house is filled with Elizabethan furniture and early pictures. There is a spectacular gallery, more than 160 feet (49 metres) long, which would have been used originally to display family portraits, and the spacious great hall is much as it would have been in the early 17th century. No Elizabethan gentleman would be content without a great hall, for it showed his friends and colleagues that he was a man of means.

The house contains a remarkable work by England's greatest animal painter, George Stubbs (1724–1806). Working just from the skin – since no live example had ever been seen in Europe at that time – Stubbs produced what is almost certainly Britain's first likeness of a kangaroo.

Below: Elizabethan Parham House, although open to the public, is still a family home, too. It contains the earliest known painting by an English artist of a kangaroo.

The gardens, including the 300-acre (121.5-hectare) deer park, are equally fascinating. The herd of fallow deer is made up of descendants of animals introduced here in the 1620s and the 7-acre (2.8-hectare) pleasure garden – an 18th-century creation – has a lake, rare trees and a wonderful brick-and-turf maze.

St Botolph's Church
Hardham, West Sussex

Almost every aspect of church-going today would have been unfamiliar to our medieval ancestors. If you want to see what pretty much every parish church in the country would have looked like before Henry VIII (1491–1547) fell out with the Pope, you must visit this tiny church.

St Botolph's is largely Norman, and is very small because, more than 900 years ago, this was a remote and very poor rural community. The importance of the church, however, can be judged by its superb wall paintings.

Other churches have more spectacular individual wall paintings, but none has retained virtually all its original work. At St Botolph's almost every surface – from the sides of the nave to the chancel arch and the altar – is covered with beautifully executed scenes from the Life of Christ. There are also extraordinary pictures of Adam and Eve, including one of Eve milking a cow. Another shows the serenity of heaven and the horrors of hell. The Apostles are portrayed, as is St George slaying the dragon.

These extraordinary works of art were painted to instruct an illiterate population. It is believed that St Botolph's images were the work of a group of painters employed around 1100 to wander the country painting such scenes. Before the Reformation of the 16th century, most churches in England would have contained comparable work and it is ironic that the whitewash that eventually covered these pictures actually helped preserve them for our benefit today.

Below: St Botolph's Church has retained almost all its original wall paintings, which were designed to tell biblical stories to an illiterate population.

CISSBURY RING
Near Findon, West Sussex

It's easy to understand why ancient people built a hill fort on this high chalk promontory on the South Downs, with its breathtaking views across to the Isle of Wight and to Beachy Head.

When the valleys were dangerous, thickly wooded places, it made sense to build forts on these high tops. What remains of the Cissbury Iron Age hill fort is still impressive today, thousands of years after it was first built: the ancient ditch and ramparts enclose over 65 acres (26 hectares), suggesting that this was a strategically important place. The inner ring alone is over a mile (1.6km) long.

Beneath the hill, evidence of earlier peoples has been found. Stone Age tribes, using only antler picks, dug shafts – some as deep as 40 feet (12 metres) – and tunnels here in search of flint.

Sixty thousand tons of chalk must have been moved to build the inner bank, but some time between 50 BC and AD 50 the fort was abandoned forever. Soon the timber palisades and huts would have crumbled and vanished, leaving only the earthworks we see today.

Above: The ancient ditch of Cissbury Ring once enclosed a strategically important hill fort and some 65 acres (26 hectares) of downland.

For the modern visitor there are a wealth of natural history pleasures to be found here: rare grassland plants, such as cowslip and horseshoe vetch, butterflies, such as the chalkhill blue, and several wonderful species of orchid – look out for the pyramidal orchid in particular.

Lovely but lonely, the view from the hill fort on a clear day will give you a glimpse of the impressive spire of Salisbury Cathedral in Wiltshire or along the coast to the promontory of Selsey Bill in the misty distance.

CHYNGTON FARM
Alfriston, East Sussex

If you head east from the ancient port of Seaford on the Sussex coast, you soon reach the Cuckmere estuary with its ancient saltmarsh and wetland. The estuary has no modern coastal town or urban development of any kind, making it unique among the south-coast rivers. Close to where the river meanders into the sea is Chyngton Farm. Chyngton gets its name from the settlement – of which nothing now remains – that existed here in the Middle Ages, before the Black Death and the growth of Seaford led to its being abandoned.

Above: Legend has it that Mad Jack Fuller is buried in the pyramid he built in the early 19th century.

The National Trust, aware of the rarity of this quiet, unspoiled landscape in the busiest corner of England, manages the land. Controlled incursion of the sea has regenerated the typical saltmarsh environment that is now home to thousands of wading birds and duck – from plover to curlew, redshank, widgeon, teal and mallard. Songbirds are also abundant – particularly yellowhammer – and high in the skies you are likely to see a number of birds of prey, including sparrowhawk, peregrine falcon and kestrel.

The farm is criss-crossed by water-filled ditches which support countless species of insect, including jewel-bright dragonflies and damselflies, while down at the very edge of the sea on the shingle bank there are rare plants, such as sea kale and sea lavender. This ancient and wildlife-rich site is easily reached from the Seven Sisters Country Park, and is part of the Seaford to Beachy Head Site of Special Scientific Interest.

Those who walk the nearby South Downs Way often miss this hidden valley and its remarkable ecosystem. Chyngton is also believed to have been the last farm in England to use oxen to pull carts and ploughs. Photographs taken in the 1930s showed the ox teams still at work, as they would have been in earlier centuries.

JACK FULLER'S PYRAMID
Brightling, East Sussex

The village of Brightling, with its surrounding beech woods, lies in one of the loveliest parts of Sussex. It was here that 'Mad' Jack Fuller (1757–1834), the son of minor gentry, inherited Brightling Park.

Though he shunned publicity and even refused a knighthood, Fuller was determined not to be forgotten. In the manner of the ancient Egyptians, he thought that one way to ensure his immortality was to build a pyramid – so that's precisely what he did. But, not content with a pyramid, he also built a steeple and two domes.

The pyramid in Brightling churchyard is the most interesting of Fuller's follies. The work was supervised by Sir Robert Smirke, the architect of the British Museum, and measures 25 feet (8 metres) high and 80 feet (24 metres) round the base. Carefully constructed from large, precision-cut blocks of stone, it was completed in 1811 as Fuller's mausoleum, decades before he died. The pyramid is believed (though the story is apocryphal) to contain his mummified body, sitting bolt upright in a chair!

Fuller, who later became a Member of Parliament, was considered highly eccentric even in his own lifetime. He built a stone obelisk, Brightling Needle, which stands over 40 feet (12 metres) high, on a nearby hill. A smaller obelisk, the Sugar Loaf, was planned to trick a neighbour into believing that Fuller could see the church spire at Dallington. Fuller couldn't see it, so he built the Sugar Loaf just within sight and in the general direction of Dallington, simply to fool his colleague.

In Brightling Park Fuller built what is now known as the Watch Tower (so he could keep an eye on restoration work at nearby Bodiam Castle), a summer house in the style of a Greek temple, and an observatory. The pyramid, however, is undoubtedly his most remarkable legacy.

BATEMAN'S
Burwash, East Sussex

Rudyard Kipling lived at Bateman's from 1902 until the end of his life in 1936, and when you first see the richly coloured sandstone house, which was built in 1634, it is easy to see why he favoured it. It is a small house – never owned by a grand or titled family, but precisely because of that, a rare survivor.

Bateman's was built for a local ironmaster, well off but by no means aristocratic, and its most striking feature is the extraordinary six-column central chimney stack.

Kipling tried to make the interior look as it would have done when the house was first built. He filled it with early furniture, including his own 17th-century writing table and artefacts collected from the country that inspired so much of his writing: India. He made sure his book-lined study – his workroom – was situated right at

Right: Rudyard Kipling's Sussex home, Bateman's, was built in the early 17th century. It still houses many of the great man's treasures, including his pipes and his Rolls Royce.

the middle of the house at the top of the main staircase. Here he wrote *If* and, among other stories and poems, *Puck of Pook's Hill*.

Pens, pipes, and even Kipling's Rolls Royce are still here. In the garden can still be found the shallow-bottomed pond he built so that visitors, including his friends' children, could bathe and go boating. A tradition grew up that guests, where necessary, should put 'FIP' after their names in the visitors' book: it stood for 'Fell In Pond'.

Kipling also laid out the rose garden and planted a yew hedge. His wife left the house to the National Trust in 1939 with a stipulation that it should be kept as her husband had known it. The inscription on Kipling's sundial is typical of his humour: 'It is later than you think.'

THE MERMAID INN

Rye, East Sussex

Though the sea on which it once relied for trade has long ago retreated, the ancient town of Rye still thrives – and deservedly so, for this is one of the most untouched places in England.

Approached from the east across the bleak, windswept beauty of Romney Marsh, Rye reveals an outline that still has a distinctly medieval air about it and, indeed, the town is best known for its remarkable number of ancient buildings.

Tucked away among these, and older than most, is The Mermaid Inn, from which the town's main street gets its name. Originally built in 1156, the Mermaid was substantially rebuilt in 1420, but – and this is what makes it so special – it has hardly been touched since.

Appropriately enough for an inn built in a seafarers' town, the Mermaid is con-structed largely from ships' timbers and it is said that when storms rock the house the ghostly crash of waves can still be heard from the crooked bedrooms.

At the bottom of Mermaid Street (formerly Middle Street) and just off the quay, the sea once offered sailors an anchorage 20 feet (6 metres) deep at high tide. There was space for more than a hundred ships, which may also explain the Mermaid's long-standing reputation as a haunt of smugglers.

Opposite: The Mermaid Inn at Rye was built from ships' timbers early in the 15th century and looks today much as it would have done then, when it was a popular haunt of smugglers.

Right: St Augustine's Church, whose detached octagonal bell tower leans at a crazy angle, has stood the test of time – it was built in the 13th century – remarkably well.

ST AUGUSTINE'S CHURCH

Brookland, Kent

St Augustine's Church lies at the heart of the small, neatly ordered village of Brookland in the heart of Walland Marsh. The nearest town is Tenterden, some 12 miles (20km) to the north. The most striking thing about this unusual church is that its bell tower is detached. It is also octagonal, with a conical timber roof, and is certainly contemporary with the rest of the 13th-century structure.

When standing in the nave of the church you will feel decidedly wobbly, for this part of the building – notice particularly the nave arches – leans out at an impossible angle. As with the leaning Tower of Pisa in Italy, no one really knows why the church has not collapsed. The fact that it hasn't, and is apparently in no danger of doing so, is a cause of celebration.

On the south wall there is a splendid painting of the great Kentish martyr St Thomas à Becket (c. 1118–70). The nave successfully escaped the Victorian mania for 'improving' ancient churches and St Augustine's also retains its beautiful Georgian box pews and pulpit.

The church also has a unique font that is arguably the most extraordinary anywhere in Britain. Almost certainly Norman, it shows the signs of the zodiac together with their accompanying symbols. Its exact significance and origin are unknown; it is a fascinating mystery.

DEREK JARMAN'S GARDEN
Dungeness, Kent

Best known as an artist and film-maker, Derek Jarman (1942–94) came to this remote (some would say bleak) corner of Kent during the last years of his life. Round his tiny Prospect Cottage, which faces out across the vast sea of shingle towards a huge, futuristic-looking power station, he created a remarkable contemporary garden.

If you decide to visit, you must divest your mind of the normal conceptions of gardens and gardening, for Derek Jarman created his outdoor space from objects picked up on the beach – flotsam and jetsam – and the garden is all the more interesting for that. More like a sculpture or art installation, the garden mixes the finds of a beachcomber with stones and a few salt-tolerant plants.

Below: Using flotsam and driftwood – and his imagination – the artist and film-maker Derek Jarman (1942–94) created a remarkable modern garden on the bleak, windswept shingle at Dungeness.

ST LEONARD'S CHURCH
Hythe, Kent

The wall paintings are long gone and the dark, dusty corners of even our oldest churches were long ago swept clean, whitewashed and made suitable for coffee mornings and weddings.

But one or two churches hidden away in obscure parts of the country retain something of their dark, pre-Reformation past. One such is St Leonard's Church, where thousands of human bones are still stored – as in medieval times – in a charnel house.

Although it is probably fair to say that most charnel houses were in the churchyard, some churches did keep the bones in an unused chapel. At St Leonard's the charnel house has always been under the chancel in the crypt. This is strange in itself, as a crypt would normally allow entrance to the main body of the church and this one does not. The likely explanation is that the St Leonard's crypt is an ambulatory: a consecrated route round the church for processions of one kind or another.

Today, the crypt, or ambulatory, houses more than 8000 thigh bones and 2000 skulls. All have been dated to the early Middle Ages and have survived because conditions in the crypt are – quite by chance – ideal for their preservation.

Eerily, some of the skulls show signs of trepanning – the surgical practice of cutting holes in the skull to release pressure. Archaeologists believe that the operation was carried out on people suffering some

sort of mental illness. Judging by signs of healing, it looks as if the individuals whose trepanned skulls finally ended up in St Leonard's lived to tell the tale!

The rest of the church is equally fascinating. The archway to St Edmund's chapel is clearly Saxon, but the Normans added on to the original tiny chapel; a nave was built in 1080 and the aisles were added early in the 12th century. The only substantially altered part of this remarkable building is the tower, which was rebuilt in 1750 after the original collapsed in an earthquake.

As befits an ancient port, representations of fishing vessels are carved on the church walls.

THE GRAND SHAFT

Dover, Kent

Three clockwise staircases, one above the other, rise up from Dover's Snargate Street through a 26-foot-diameter (8-metre) shaft cut through the cliffs to the Western Heights, the cliff-top defences built to protect England against invasion during the Napoleonic Wars (1796–1815).

Hidden from view, the Grand Shaft – as the triple staircase is known – was built to allow troops to get from town to their defensive positions as quickly as possible. Before its construction the soldiers had to clamber down steep, chalky trackways that were treacherous during bad weather.

The Grand Shaft was the brainchild of Brigadier General Twiss. He suggested it in 1804 and the shaft was completed in 1809. Brick-lined, with an occasional window for light and steps made at great expense from Purbeck limestone, it rises some 140 feet (43 metres).

The three staircases were required because the class structure of England was so rigid in the early 19th century that officials could not bear the idea that officers and men should use the same steps. One staircase is labelled 'officers and their ladies', another is marked 'sergeants and their wives' and a third for 'soldiers and their women'. All three met at a short sloping stretch at the bottom of the tunnel that led down to the barred entrance in Snargate Street.

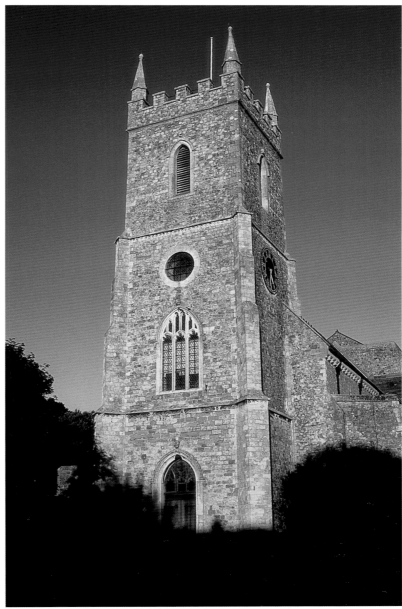

Above: St Leonard's Church, with its bone-filled charnel house, retains a dark, pre-Reformation atmosphere.

Snargate Street dates back to the 15th century, at which time it was actually on the beach, and the cliffs nearby are riddled with tunnels, old storehouses and hidden cellars. Many more probably remain undiscovered.

When the threatened Napoleonic invasion failed to happen, the Grand Shaft gradually became disused – except by soldiers heading from the cliff-top barracks to the beach to bathe – until it was restored in the 1980s. It is open only during the summer.

CAMBRIDGESHIRE, ESSEX, SUFFOLK & NORFOLK

Famed for its ancient villages, windmills and medieval churches, East Anglia is also a place of wild beaches, prehistoric remains, forgotten woodlands, abbeys, follies and towers.

KEY
1. Flag Fen Bronze Age Centre
2. Wicken Fen
3. Anglesey Abbey
4. Wimpole Hall and Farm
5. St Andrew's Church
6. Thrift Wood
7. St Peter on the Wall
8. Layer Marney Tower
9. Tattingstone Wonder
10. Ickworth House
11. The Nutshell
12. Welney Wildfowl Reserve
13. Church of St Peter and St Paul
14. Blickling Hall
15. Little Walsingham
16. Blakeney Point

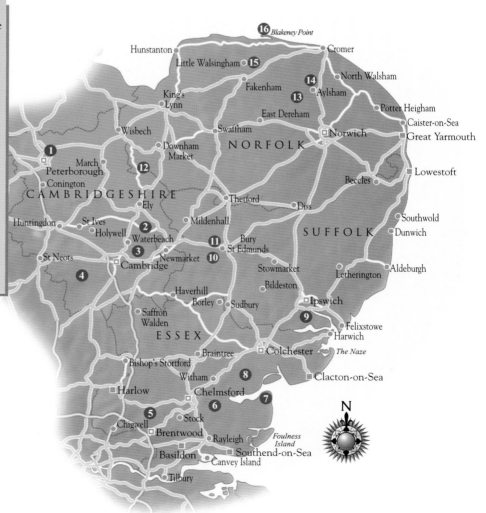

FLAG FEN BRONZE AGE CENTRE

Near Peterborough, Cambridgeshire

The stone and earthwork remains of pre-literate peoples in England – Stonehenge, Avebury and so on – represent only a small fraction of the structures and artefacts that would have been made perhaps 3000 or more years ago. There is no doubt that these ancient people, about whom we know so little, made many of their buildings, tools, boats and utensils from timber, a material that rarely survived long enough to be discovered by modern archaeologists.

Very occasionally we find vestiges of their extraordinary woodworking skills in odd fragments in waterlogged sites, but it is very rare indeed to find a major site with large amounts of prehistoric wooden technology intact. Yet that is just what was unearthed at Flag Fen. Discovered as recently as 1982, Flag Fen is a remarkable place: a wooden platform the size of a modern football pitch was built here around 3000 BC, and some 60,000 timber posts in alignment were driven into the ground. Yet we have almost no idea why this work was carried out – at what must have been great expense in terms of time and labour.

At Flag Fen, visitors can see archaeology in action, as day by day researchers are discovering things for the first time about our ancient ancestors. As a result of the work at Flag Fen, many long-held views about England's early population have had to be revised.

The timbers at Flag Fen have been so well preserved in the waterlogged conditions of the fen that archaeologists can even determine the type of axes that were used to fell the trees, how many of them were probably

Above: A recreated Bronze Age house at Flag Fen. Masses of carved and shaped timbers have been found at this site, which was clearly of enormous significance for the ancient tribe that once inhabited this part of the fens.

used, as well as details of how the logs were split using wedges and then shaped.

The museum at Flag Fen has on display the oldest wooden wheel ever found in England, together with other remarkable timber artefacts.

WICKEN FEN
Wicken, Cambridgeshire

A huge area of what is today East Anglia was once a forbidding wetland. Right across Cambridgeshire, Norfolk and Lincolnshire the land was permanently flooded and only the local people knew the routes through the treacherous bog and marsh. The locals made a living catching eels and other fish in hand-made baskets and trapped wildfowl in winter.

Then came the Dutch engineers: the marshes were drained, the floods began to recede and one of the greatest wildlife habitats in the world – an area that was once home to millions of birds, insects and mammals – became the flat empty farmland we see today. Just a few tiny pockets of the old fen still exist, hidden amid tens of thousands of acres of arable land. The best of these is undoubtedly Wicken Fen.

Wicken is also Britain's oldest nature reserve and is now run by the National Trust. It was probably the Victorians' enthusiasm for collecting insects that saved Wicken from the draining that destroyed the rest of the fens: the great natural historian Charles Darwin (1809–82), among others, came here on several insect-collecting trips.

The reserve now covers more than 800 acres (324 hectares) and traditional fen practices, such as reed harvesting and peat cutting, have produced an extraordinarily rich waterscape. Some 30 species of mammal, more than 200 species of birds, 25 species of dragonfly, 1000 different species of beetle and well over 100 species of moths and butterflies have been recorded here. Many of these species are endangered, some critically so.

ANGLESEY ABBEY
Lode, Cambridgeshire

We don't know exactly when Anglesey Abbey was founded, but it was almost certainly during the reign of Henry I (1068–1135). By the mid-13th century, the abbey was a thriving community. When Henry VIII (1491–1547) closed it in 1535 the building was not entirely demolished and some of it was turned into a Tudor house.

Today, the house retains much of the original Augustinian monastery, including the chapter house and monk's parlour. Above the entrance to the house, a Latin inscription boldly includes the line: 'This building was founded for religious purposes in the reign of Henry I and destroyed by the eighth ruler of the same name.'

During the 17th century, the house was owned by the Parker family. One member of this family was the wealthy carter Thomas Hobson, from whom we derive the phrase 'Hobson's Choice' – Hobson required every customer to take either the horse nearest the stable door or none at all.

The house was also owned for a time by Sir George

Opposite above: Anglesey Abbey is a former monastic foundation that was transformed into a beautiful house.

Left: The wetland landscape of Wicken Fen is a reminder of how much of the vast flat East Anglian landscape once looked like.

Downing, developer of London's famous Downing Street, and then in 1926 by the extraordinary Huttleston Broughton, or Lord Fairhaven. Broughton housed his huge collection of antiques here, and set about transforming the 100-acre (40-hectare) garden into 22 distinct areas. These included a symmetrical formal garden, lawns, avenues of trees, one of England's finest collections of garden statuary, snowdrop walks, a dahlia garden, a pinetum and a gorgeous arboretum with oak, horse chestnut and lime trees.

WIMPOLE HALL AND FARM
Arrington, Cambridgeshire

Wimpole is the biggest country house in Cambridgeshire. Set in more than 2500 acres (1000 hectares), the house was built in 1640 (it replaced an ancient moated house) and, as with so many English country houses, it has been added to over the centuries.

In the case of Wimpole, the architects and landscape gardeners who worked on the house or park over the

Right: Classical figures adorn Wimpole Hall, Cambridgeshire's largest country house.

centuries were among the greatest we have ever produced, and included James Gibbs (1682–1754), the ubiquitous Lancelot 'Capability' Brown (1716–83), Henry Flitcroft (1697–1769), Humphrey Repton (1752–1818) and the great Sir John Soane (1753–1837), who built the beautiful bath-house, the bookroom and the extraordinary yellow drawing room.

Much of the furniture in the house was collected by Mrs Elsie Bambridge, who bought the house in the 1930s and filled it the kind of furniture and pictures it would have had when the earls of Hardwicke owned the house in the late 18th century.

The remains of three medieval villages which were destroyed to create the view from the house can still be seen as bumps and hollows in the landscape. These and the outlines of long-vanished lanes combine to make any walk through the grounds a ghostly experience.

In addition to the fascinating house and grounds is Wimpole Farm. The farm was established more than two centuries ago and is now home to some of Britain's rarest breeds of farm animal, including Leicester longwool sheep, Gloucester old spot pigs and bagot goats.

St Andrew's Church
Near Chipping Ongar, Essex

Timber, the favoured building material of Vikings and Saxons, does not last – which may explain why in many cases we know far more about the architecture of the Romans, who built largely in stone in Britain, than about the timber-building invaders of the Dark Ages.

But just outside Chipping Ongar, concealed down an unlikely looking track, stands what is almost certainly the oldest wooden church in the world.

The walls of this small church are made from whole split oak-tree trunks, which were probably incorporated into the building in the 11th century. Other parts of the church have been dated to as early 650 AD. The Normans and Tudors added to the building, and it has been restored and refitted many times over the years, but for some reason those massive oak walls were never replaced.

The curved side of each split log faces outward, leaving the flat sides to create a more or less even surface on the inside of the church.

THRIFT WOOD

Bicknacre, near Maldon, Essex

Ancient woodland is now very rare indeed in lowland England, which makes the survival of Thrift Wood all the more remarkable. Here, against all the odds, you will find almost 50 acres (20 hectares) of centuries-old oak alongside coppiced hornbeam, ash, chestnut and birch trees. The wood is also home to the heath fritillary butterfly, which became extinct in Essex in the early 1980s but was subsequently reintroduced.

Coppicing – the periodic cutting of wood to ensure a steady growth – is still carried out here, as it was in earlier centuries, and this management technique actually makes the site more attractive to a number of bird and plant species. Among a wide range of common and not so common birds are warblers and three species of woodpecker. A murky pond surrounded by boggy ground provides a home for various amphibians, as well as numerous species of moss, spearwort and sedge.

The trackways through the wood are thought to be sections of medieval green lanes. This area has never been ploughed, so as you wander through it you will be seeing Essex much as it might have looked to a traveller in the Middle Ages, when the county was one of the most heavily wooded regions of the country. It was from here that the oaks were cut to build the fleet that defeated the Spanish Armada in 1588. Today, only rare, hidden fragments such as this remain to remind us of what we have lost.

ST PETER ON THE WALL

Bradwell-on-Sea, Essex

If there were a prize for the loneliest building in England, St Peter on the Wall might well win it.

Miles from any house, St Peter on the Wall stands at the mouth of the River Blackwater. It was built as a cathedral by St Cedd in about 650 AD on the foundations of a Roman fort (it was just 200 years after the Romans had left Britain). What we see today is only the chapel, but throughout the Dark Ages the chapel would have been just one of a small group of monastic buildings.

When the wind hurtles in from the North Sea this is a bitter place, but St Cedd had travelled to Essex from the world-famous monastery on Lindisfarne in the even colder and more windswept northern county of Northumberland, so this wild place would probably have felt like home to him.

Even today there is a long walk from the nearest road to reach the chapel, but this is part of the obscure charm of the place. Little is left inside the chapel to tell of its extraordinary 1400-year life, but the fact that it was emptied and used as a barn for centuries is probably the only reason it survived at all.

Opposite: The walls of St Andrew's Church are made from split oak trunks. Though much of the rest of the church has been restored, the walls have stood, it is thought, since the 11th century.

Below: Far away over the now uninhabited landscape, the Saxon Chapel of St Peter on the Wall was built on the foundations of a Roman fort.

LAYER MARNEY TOWER
Colchester, Essex

Visitors to Layer Marney often express sadness that the rest of the house appears to have been demolished, but in fact it was never built. The huge gatehouse or tower – which is the tallest Tudor gatehouse in the country at nearly 80 feet (24 metres) – was originally intended as part of a courtyard house that was never built.

The extraordinary tower and the planned house were commissioned by the first Lord Marney in the early part of the 16th century, but he died before the project could be completed.

Layer Marney is actually a twin tower, with a gatehouse above the entrance in between the two towers. It has eight stories of windows, is made from small, beautiful hand-made bricks and is covered in heraldic and other carvings, which include dolphins and angels in gorgeous terracotta.

Today, although still privately owned, the tower is open to the public. Visitors may climb the narrow, winding staircase for a spectacular view across the wide, flat landscape.

TATTINGSTONE WONDER
Near Ipswich, Suffolk

This is without question one of the most wonderfully eccentric buildings in the country. Originally two red-brick farmworkers' cottages, the buildings were transformed when local landowner Edward White decided he wanted a better, more religious view from his house, Tattingstone Place. So, in 1790, White built a third cottage on the end of the first two, with a fake square, flint church tower on top.

What makes this group of buildings so bizarre, is that White only built three sides to his fake steeple. He couldn't see the southern wall from his home, so, from his point of view (literally) there was no point building one, after all, the wall's absence didn't affect his 'medieval church experience'!

ICKWORTH HOUSE
Horringer, Suffolk

Frederick Hervey (1730–1803), Bishop of Derry and 4th Earl of Bristol, was an obsessive traveller and collector who built Ickworth House simply to have somewhere to put his vast collection of treasures.

Hervey's eccentric journeys through Europe help explain the number of 'Hotel Bristols' that still exist in cities all over Europe – the hotels were keen to advertise that the wealthy aristocrat and prelate had been a customer. The wandering bishop and earl, who was noted for his fondness

Left: The huge gateway that dominates the buildings at Layer Marney is, at nearly 80 feet (24 metres), Britain's tallest Tudor tower.

Opposite: The bizarre cluster of buildings known as the Tattingstone Wonder gave a local resident a religious outlook while retaining a little housing.

for leap-frogging over the backs of lesser ecclesiastics, poured much of his dotty personality into Ickworth.

Basing his designs on Italian architecture, Hervey had Ickworth built with a central rotunda and two big curving wings. What most concerned him was not that the house should be comfortable for people to live in but that it should provide a suitable setting for his collection of paintings by Velázquez, Titian and Gainsborough.

The pictures, along with his other collections – most notably of exquisite Georgian silver and fine Regency furniture – remain at the house to this day.

The gardens, however, would not be familiar to Hervey, as they were created in the early 19th century by the 1st Marquis of Bristol. It was he who created the Victorian Stumpery and the Temple Rose Garden, but Hervey's summer house and ornamental canal survive.

Beyond the gardens lie the wooded park, without which no self-respecting 18th-century house was considered complete.

Below: Ickworth, with its huge central dome, was built by the eccentric Bishop of Derry – a man more famous for travel and collecting than for piety.

THE NUTSHELL
Bury St Edmunds, Suffolk

Whatever the claims of various pubs to be either the oldest, the biggest or the smallest in the country, there is no doubt that the Nutshell is a very small pub indeed. Although the pub is built on three floors, the drinking area measures just 15 feet by 7 feet (4.5 metres by 2 metres) – that's just 100 square feet (30.5 square metres) of drinking space! Despite its size, the pub once managed to achieve a new world record by squeezing 102 customers and a dog into the bar.

On the other hand, it is not too small to provide a permanent home to its very own ghost: a little boy who is believed to have been murdered several centuries ago is regularly spotted flitting up or down the stairs towards closing time. However, the pub is not actually very old, and is believed to have been erected in the early 19th century. The pub is owned by local brewers Greene King, so be sure to try a pint when you visit.

The Guinness Book of Records accepts the Nutshell's claim to be the smallest pub in the country and, in

keeping with the spirit of commercialism, the pub now houses the world's smallest dartboard as well as, bizarrely, a stuffed three-legged chicken and a mummified cat.

WELNEY WILDFOWL RESERVE

Welney, Norfolk

Welney was once the centre of a wildfowl-hunting culture that dated back to man's first arrival at this flooded, forbidding corner of England. Early settlers lived by duck and goose, as a local saying has it, particularly in winter when the meres were frozen and a little money could be raised by taking waterfowl to market.

Even into the early part of the 20th century, the old 'puntgunners' worked the marshes here: lying face down in their flat canoes, they would drift within range of a raft of teal or tufted duck before firing their huge blunderbuss-like guns at the flocks of birds.

Above: Welney, where the marshes were worked by punt-gunners in the 19th century, is now home to vast numbers of wildfowl, many of which overwinter here.

Above left: The public drinking area of The Nutshell measures just 15 feet by 7 feet (4.5 metres by 2 metres), thus qualifying it as the Smallest Pub in England.

Today, Welney, that strip of the Washes between the Old and New Bedford rivers which floods each winter, is still an extraordinarily rich place for waders and wildfowl, and indeed for those who come to watch and study them rather than shoot them.

Winter is the best time to visit, as this is when the hordes of migrating birds escape the worst of the Arctic winter and arrive here in their tens of thousands. The list of species you are likely to see is almost endless: among the ducks there are pintail, shoveller, pochard, wigeon and teal, and among the geese are pinkfoot and greylag; grebes and Bewick's swans also come here.

CHURCH OF ST PETER AND ST PAUL

Salle, Norfolk

In a sense, England is awash with remarkable hidden churches. They can be found down lost lanes in out-of-the-way places or concealed behind later monolithic developments. But here, between the villages of Reepham and Cawston, in a county blessed with far more than its fair share of remarkable churches, is a building that offers a dazzling array of medieval craftsmanship.

Wherever you look there are carvings in the 15th-century stone and woodwork – dragons and monkeys can be found on the misericords beneath the oak choir seats, along with flowers, bunches of grapes and swans.

Why the medieval craftsmen made these images in a place they would rarely be seen (beneath the tip-up seats) remains a mystery. They may be connected with the medieval idea of the bestiary; whatever strange creature man could imagine or create was somehow seen as a further testiment to the glory of God.

The armrests at the Church of St Peter and St Paul are especially beautifully, with their strange carved creatures – apes and monsters predominate, but these have strange additions, such as webbed feet.

High above, the ancient timber roof is equally profusely carved – here, if you have sharp eyes, you will notice numerous wooden angels and beautifully carved bosses.

Bizzarely, given that churches are supposed to be welcoming, the doors to the church are guarded on either side by fierce-looking creatures carrying heavy clubs. They are known as 'wodewoses' and echo older pagan creatures.

Above: The Church of St Peter and St Paul at Salle is a repository of some of the greatest medieval craftsmanship in the country.

Opposite and opposite above: Multi-gabled and imposing, Blickling Hall is a superb example of Jacobean architecture, and is rich in elaborate decorative detail.

BLICKLING HALL

Blickling, Norfolk

In that disastrous period for the English country house between the two world wars, dozens of beautiful buildings were demolished. Norfolk suffered as much in this respect as any other county in England, if not more, partly because in medieval times it was such a wealthy county. Rich merchants spent their money on churches and houses, and though the greatest of these survive, those owned by the less famous fared worse.

Blickling Hall is an impressive house, but its chief claim to fame in earlier times was that it replaced the house in which Anne Boleyn (1507–36) was born.

Perhaps because it was too far from London for its owner to wield great political influence, it has an almost homely air.

Hidden away inside the house, however, is the most spectacular plaster ceiling, which runs the whole length of the Long Gallery – almost 130 feet (40 metres) in all. The ceiling is covered with allegorical figures, together with representations of the five senses, with flowers and swirls of almost dazzling intricacy.

In a sense, the Long Gallery ceiling is not so much a monument to the wealthy individual who commissioned it as to the extraordinary skills of the workmen who created it.

Blickling's other claim to fame are the fabulous ancient yews that

The splendid multi-gabled house that has come down to us is a classic example of Jacobean architecture. It's a big house, but has nothing of the imposing grandeur of, say, Hatfield or Burghley. line the way to the front of the house, and the Chinese bedroom where the walls still carry the hand-painted Chinese wallpaper that was hung in the 18th century.

LITTLE WALSINGHAM

Near Fakenham, Norfolk

Walsingham has been a place of pilgrimage for Catholics since the Middle Ages. The original shrine of Our Lady of Walsingham was founded as early as 1061. It was then destroyed during the Reformation of the 16th century and not re-established until 1934. Walsingham is now more popular than ever, and still largely as a place for the religious to visit, but the village has much of interest for the general visitor.

Despite the fact that little of medieval Walsingham

Below: A place of pilgrimage since the Middle Ages, Little Walsingham is an attractive village in its own right.

remains, the place has a curiously ancient feel to it. There's something almost eccentric about the place. For example, the former train station has an onion dome on its roof, the work of a Russian Orthodox monk who came here in the 1960s and sought permission to turn the disused building into a chapel.

You have to leave Walsingham to find a truly ancient place, but if you do make the journey to the Slipper Chapel in nearby Houghton St Giles you you will be following in the footsteps of medieval pilgrims. The chapel, which is largely 14th-century, gets its name from the fact that pilgrims to Walsingham would stop here before tackling the last mile or so of their journey, and here they would remove their shoes so that this last part could be completed in a suitably pious, and undoubtedly painful, condition.

BLAKENEY POINT

Near Langham, Norfolk

The whole of the Norfolk coast might justly be termed a bird sanctuary, for everywhere the marshes and creeks, sands and inlets are filled with birds of all species.

But Blakeney Point, lonely and remote though it might be, is truly special. It's a simple shingle spit some 3½ miles (5.75km) long, but that narrow space is one of the great secrets of Norfolk. This bleak promontory has been thrown up, created as if from nothing by centuries of wave action.

You can take a ferry to the point itself, but it's more fun – and far more bracing – to walk out along the narrow windswept spit; when there is a big sea running and the wind is up it is a most exhilarating experience. You will soon realize, too, why it's so popular with sailing dinghy enthusiasts.

At the point where the sea has created a wider place of sand and shingle, huge numbers of migrating birds make this their first landfall.

As well as birds, the point is also hugely popular with seals, which rest on the pebbles amid the thousands of geese and ducks. The point is a major site for nesting terns and for twitchers, those fanatical birdwatchers who will travel any distance to spot a rare migrant.

Below: Wild, windswept and remote, Blakeney Point is a creation of the sea and the storms that sweep down the Norfolk coast from the Arctic.

NORTHAMPTONSHIRE, RUTLAND, LEICESTERSHIRE, NOTTINGHAMSHIRE & LINCOLNSHIRE

From round churches to old bell-making firms, from yew drives to medieval crosses, these ancient counties are rich in offbeat places ~ including what is probably the oldest domestic building in Britain.

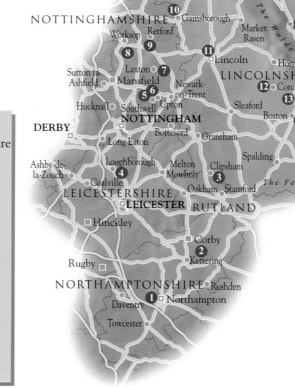

KEY

1. Church of the Holy Sepulchure
2. Eleanor Cross
3. The Clipsham Yews
4. Loughborough Bell Foundry and Museum
5. Southwell Workhouse
6. Upton Hall Time Museum
7. Laxton
8. Clumber Park
9. Mr Straw's House
10. Gainsborough Old Hall
11. The Jew's House
12. Tattershall Castle
13. Sibsey Trader Windmill
14. Maud Foster Mill

CHURCH OF THE HOLY SEPULCHRE

Northampton, Northamptonshire

In some ways it is a pity that almost all the best architecture that survives from the Middle Ages and earlier is ecclesiastical. Domestic buildings dating from before AD 1400 (and in a largely unaltered state) are extremely rare. On the other hand, early churches do provide evidence of the skills and ideas of a long-vanished people that would almost certainly have been reflected to some extent in other buildings. Among the rarest and most interesting medieval buildings are the round churches.

Only four of these survive in England. The least altered, though much added to, is the Church of the Holy Sepulchre in Northampton. The 1st Earl of Northampton, Simon de Senlis, built it in 1100, after he returned from one of the great medieval crusades to Jerusalem.

That de Senlis survived what must, at the time, have been an incredibly dangerous journey is remarkable enough, but far more amazing is his recreation of Jerusalem's own Church of the Holy Sepulchre. This is a very close replica, and on entry it is easy to believe that you have suddenly been transported to the Middle East.

Just inside the entrance, de Senlis created a sunken circular space supported by 16 pillars. This was originally the nave, but a long chancel was added in the 13th century, together with the spire and tower at the end of the 14th century. The Victorian architect George Gilbert Scott added the apse in 1838.

The fact that the church was built in a recognizably Middle Eastern style is revealing. There was an obsession during the Middle Ages – certainly among the aristocracy – with reclaiming Jerusalem for European Christianity. If the crusaders could not ultimately hold Jerusalem, at least de Senlis was able to create something of Jerusalem in the English countryside.

ELEANOR CROSS

Geddington, Northamptonshire

When Edward I's queen, Eleanor of Castile, died in 1290, her coffin was carried from Harby in Nottinghamshire to London's Westminster Abbey. In each of the places the cortège stopped to overnight on the long journey south, Edward later erected a cross to commemorate his dead queen. Only three of the original dozen crosses survive, and the best is that at Geddington.

Below: Geddington's Eleanor Cross is one of 12 such crosses erected to commemorate the end of a great medieval romance, the marriage of Edward I with Eleanor of Castile.

The cross stands in the middle of the small village, and to most visitors looks like a long-forgotten monument of no special merit. But even after the passage of more than 700 years, close inspection reveals the remarkable quality of the carving. There are three niches, and in each is a statue of Eleanor. Above and below these, the elaborate and spectacular decorative carvings – typical of English Gothic – spread to the very tip and base of this tall, dignified structure.

THE CLIPSHAM YEWS
Near Clipsham, Rutland

The yew is not only the tree of graveyards, but is also our longest living tree, which helps explain the mythology that surrounds it. The yew is also a popular decorative tree, largely because it is a beautiful evergreen and can be clipped into all sorts of shapes. It was also the timber of choice for the English longbows that most famously defeated the French at Agincourt in 1415.

Below: The Clipsham Yews have been trimmed into various forms in a tradition that dates back more than a century.

The gardens of many grand houses in earlier centuries had yew walks and avenues, and one of the most impressive – and in its way bizarre – is at Clipsham Hall. More than 150 ancient yews line the drive to the house. During the Victorian period, for reasons no one has yet quite explained, the head gardener, Amos Alexander, was asked to trim the trees into a virtual menagerie. Here you will find elephants and horses as well as abstract shapes, battles scenes and even a moon landing; the tradition that began in the 1870s continues to this day, with new designs continually added to the collection.

LOUGHBOROUGH BELL FOUNDRY AND MUSEUM
Loughborough, Leicestershire

Bells have been made in the same way for centuries; the technology changes little. And they still have to be repaired regularly or replaced in Britain's thousands of churches, which is why bell founders tend to survive where other ancient manufacturers have long since vanished. Though it has passed through a number of

Left: Staff in contemporary dress help to recreate something of the spartan atmosphere inside Southwell Workhouse.

Below and below right: Bells have been made in Loughborough since medieval times. The Taylor family, who still run the business today, made the Great Paul bell for St Paul's Cathedral in London in 1881.

and hay are still used to form the hollow core of the bells and each one is cast by hand by skilled workmen who then shave thin slivers of metal from each bell in order to tune it. All this and more is explained in the museum, which is also devoted to hand bells, carillons and ships' bells.

families over its lifetime, the bell foundry at Loughborough, now owned by the Taylor family, has been in business continuously since the 14th century.

For centuries, bells have been sent from Taylor's all over the world. The biggest bell ever cast – the nearly 16-ton Great Paul for St Paul's Cathedral in London – was made here in 1881.

Taylors have run the business since 1784. As well as the foundry there is also a bell museum devoted to the history and mystery of the subject. Horse manure, sand

SOUTHWELL WORKHOUSE
Southwell, Nottinghamshire

Long after the workhouse had vanished as an institution, the idea of these grim, forbidding places could still strike fear into the hearts of the older generation, which is why few mourned the demolition of the hundreds of grim workhouse buildings that once dotted the urban and rural landscape.

But the workhouse was so central to the consciousness of working people that we should be grateful that – by sheer good luck – at least one workhouse building survives pretty much intact.

Built in 1824, the Southwell Workhouse provided a grim safety net for the destitute from nearly 50 parishes. It housed nearly 150 paupers, as the destitute were then known. Men and women were segregated: the men broke stones and old bones while the women unpicked old rope in return for bed and meagre board; gruel – a sort of thin porridge – was the staple food.

Today, the rooms look much as they did in the mid-19th century, and the segregated stairs – designed to make sure the sexes couldn't mix even as they moved about the building – are still there.

Below: Grand and imposing still, Southwell Workhouse was once a place that inspired fear and dread. It was built to last and has been fully restored by the National Trust.

UPTON HALL TIME MUSEUM
Upton, Nottinghamshire

What is it about clocks that so fascinates? Perhaps it is the fact that with, say, a grandfather clock, it is possible to own a beautiful piece of furniture that is also a piece of ancient technology, and one that will, moreover, still perform adequately the task for which it was first designed. Whatever the reason, clock enthusiasts will not want to miss Upton Hall, a beautiful Georgian house that is home to the British Horological Institute and its extraordinary collection of clocks, watches and timepieces.

Here you will find exquisite 17th-century longcase clocks, clocks with automata, lantern and carriage clocks, night clocks, musical clocks of staggering complexity, moon phase clocks, celestial clocks, clocks by world-famous makers such as Joseph Knibb

(1640–1711) and Thomas Tompion (*c.* 1639–1713), and even a Chinese incense clock.

Upton Hall is also home to the atomic BBC pips machine, as well as a number of clocks that are more than three centuries old.

LAXTON

Near Newark-on-Trent, Nottinghamshire

You might wonder why anyone would want to go and see 'a few fields' in the Nottinghamshire countryside at Laxton. The fact is that these are no ordinary fields; rather, they are the last remaining medieval agricultural system of land management in Britain.

Three big fields adjoin the village of Laxton, and are still, even today, ploughed in strips. At one time this agricultural system was common through-out the length and breadth of England, before enclosure in the 18th century changed the shape of the countryside forever.

Quite why Laxton alone kept to the old system is a mystery, but the three fields and the system by which they are farmed – which is first men-tioned in a document of 1200 – still have their ridge and furrow pattern of ancient times. This is the only place in the country where you can get an impres-sion of how typical medieval farmed countryside would have looked.

The Laxton Manorial Court

still meets to legislate on disputes over the strips, and visitors today can follow one of three walks that cross these rare and special fields.

Right: A splendid clock at the Upton Hall Time Museum, where you will find everything from late 17th-century longcase clocks to the BBC's atomic time machine.

CLUMBER PARK

Worksop, Nottinghamshire

At one time Clumber Park was best known, at least among those who enjoy shooting pheasants, as the place where the Clumber spaniel was first bred. This rather sorrowful looking animal is now very rare, but to own one was once the height of sophistication.

Today the park that gave the dog its name is still one of the glories of Nottinghamshire, yet Clumber is relatively little known. Perhaps this has something to do with the fact that people tend to travel through the county to get elsewhere; by doing so they miss much of what Nottinghamshire has to offer.

Below: Though the great house is long gone, the grounds of Clumber Park – with its huge carp-filled lake – are still open to the public.

Clumber Park still runs to nearly 4000 acres (1620 hectares). It is a wonder that such a huge landholding survived the rigours of inheritance tax and falling land values in the 1930s, but somehow it did. Everything about Clumber is on the biggest scale: the lime drive is over 2 miles (3km) long, and there is an 87-acre (35-hectare) lake… everything, that is, except the house.

The current condition of the house probably explains why the grounds are still intact. For Clumber House is gone. Vast and ruinously expensive to maintain, it was demolished in 1938 because the owners simply could not afford its upkeep. The house was simply dismantled: the fireplaces were sold off, the old panelling probably went to America; the furniture and pictures to Sotheby's; the stone, brick and joists to a builder's yard to be recycled for use in other, smaller, houses; and anything left unsold was eventually burned.

Above: Uniquely appealing, Mr Straw's House in Worksop is an ordinary Victorian semi-detached property caught in a time warp, a place where even the letters are half a century old.

The stable block did survive, however, and the estate is still one of Nottinghamshire's hidden gems, with mile after mile of unspoiled walks, cycle rides, bridlepaths, lakes and trees. There is one last reminder of its former glory: the kitchen garden is still intact, complete with its glasshouse, where no doubt delicate fruits such as pineapples and pomegranates were once grown for the big house.

Mr Straw's House
Worksop, Nottinghamshire

Of all the houses owned by the National Trust, this must be the most remarkable. Yet it is an ordinary semi-detached property in a not particularly attractive northern town.

Even those who live in and love Worksop would be hard pressed to put Mr Straw's House firmly on the tourist map. But no other town or city in Britain has anything to compare with it: an ordinary house unchanged in every respect since the early part of the 20th century. Grand houses and churches survive in their thousands by comparison, but ordinary semis with unaltered interiors are almost unheard of.

The story of Mr Straw's House began when a young couple moved into the house in 1923. They immediately had it done up in the most popular style of the day. But as Worksop was many miles distant from fashionable centres like London, the style is actually more like what was in vogue at the end of the 19th century. No expense was spared, from the latest linoleum, to Turkish rugs, knick-knacks, costly wallpapers and curtains.

As the years went by, the Straws changed absolutely nothing. When they died, their two sons carried on living in the house, never marrying, never removing a thing and carefully dating and labelling any new additions to the house. When the last brother died in the early 1990s he left the house and its contents to the National Trust.

Today, Mr Straw's House is exactly as it was in the early 1920s, right down to the light bulbs, runners, stair carpets and outside toilet. Even the food cupboards contain tinned items from the 1930s. The chests of drawers are filled with beautifully preserved late-Victorian linen. The brothers kept their parents' best clothes neatly folded away in cupboards and drawers and the hats and coats on the hooks in the hall have been there since 1930. To prevent everything

from fading, the brothers were careful to draw the blinds on sunny days.

The brothers must have realized that they had preserved something of great rarity, which is why they bequeathed both No. 7 Blyth Grove and the house next door, which they also owned, to the National Trust.

GAINSBOROUGH OLD HALL
Gainsborough, Lincolnshire

Tucked away in the most unassuming manner in this quiet town, Gainsborough Old Hall seems to have had luck on its side. The modernizers of the 18th century left it alone and the town planners and ring-road builders of the 1960s managed, incredibly, to miss the chance to demolish this crooked, eminently

Above: Gainsborough Old Hall survived town planners and modernizers and is now one of the most complete timber hall houses in the country.

picturesque manor house, which dates back to the 1460s.

If the survival of the building itself is a surprise, the survival of so much of the interior is not far short of miraculous. The great hall was never modernized with the insertion of a first floor and it is easy to imagine the local squire's men at long banqueting tables, the smoke from the central fire gradually wafting up through the massive oak timbers of the roof. The huge trusses and beams are still there, made from local oak cut down and shaped more than five centuries ago.

Narrow passages lead from the great hall, which echoes earlier Saxon halls, to a fabulous and atmospheric medieval kitchen, with its two massive original fireplaces.

of the flat area of Lincolnshire in which it was built.

With six floors and an overall height of nearly 75 feet (23 metres), the Sibsey Trader would have been at the cutting edge of windmill technology at the time, which may explain why it was able to struggle on as a fully working mill until as late as 1954. English Heritage restored the mill in the 1970s and 1980s, and it is now in full working order.

Sibsey is also one of the last remaining examples of the work of one of Lincolnshire's most celebrated millwrights, Saundersons of Louth.

MAUD FOSTER MILL

Boston, Lincolnshire

Despite the wholesale changes wrought by the Industrial Revolution in the 18th and 19th centuries and the introduction of modern methods of grinding corn, a surprisingly large number of wind-powered mills still exists. But even among those that have been restored, the Maud Foster Mill is a rare gem: it was built in 1819, and, almost uniquely, has five sails instead of four. Why this should be, no one knows.

The mill is also unique in that it is the tallest in Britain and the last in an area once noted for its windmills: an 18th-century traveller recalled the skyline in the Boston area as being alive with the movements and creakings of these great creatures.

But Maud Foster – the mill takes its name from one of its first owners – is no museum, or at least not entirely. In these days when we worry about the quality of our food as much as the price, the flour milled here is much in demand with regular customers right across Lincolnshire and beyond.

It's a long climb to the top of the windmill, but worth

Above: Originally with six sails (two have now been removed for safety reasons) and standing 75 feet (23 metres) high, the Sibsey Trader Windmill was at the cutting edge of technology when it was first built.

it for the views. As you descend, you can see how, at one time, all flour was produced: the intricate mechanism of cogs and pulleys, chutes and grindstones is a tribute to the craftsmen who once travelled the country constructing and repairing these vital pieces of equipment.

Shropshire, West Midlands, Staffordshire, Cheshire & Derbyshire

Covering everything from the old industrial heartland of England to more remote countryside that gazes far off to the Black Mountains of Wales, this part of Britain echoes with the ghostly sounds of 18th-century glassworks, flint mills and mining villages.

KEY

1. The Long Mynd
2. Wenlock Edge
3. Red House Glass Cone
4. Bournville
5. Soho House
6. Cannock Chase
7. Gladstone Pottery Museum
8. Cheddleton Flint Mill
9. The Salt Museum
10. Alderley Edge
11. Buxton Opera House
12. Mam Tor
13. Speedwell Cavern
14. Eyam
15. Calke Abbey

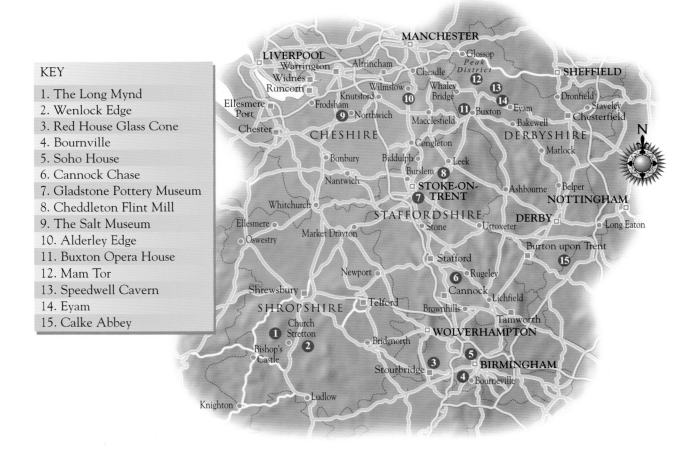

THE LONG MYND

Near Church Stretton, Shropshire

For a full 10 miles (16km) the high ridge of the Mynd cuts across Shropshire. This is one of the loveliest places in England to spend the day, and deserves to be as well known as many of the Lake District fells. There are fabulous views from the top of the ridge to Cheshire and the Black Mountains.

Hill forts were built here in ancient times, and there is evidence of human habitation from the Bronze and Iron ages right through to the Middle Ages. The ridge is cut through here and there by valleys, along which little-used tracks and pathways lead into woodlands where flycatchers and wagtails, deer and fox are left largely undisturbed.

The Mynd covers nearly 6000 acres (2430 hectares) and is designated both as an Area of Outstanding Natural Beauty and a Site of Special Scientific Interest. The soils on the Mynd are thin and acidic, once regarded as useless and unproductive, but now seen as rare and highly valued habitats for a range of species.

Above: The thin, acid soils of the Long Mynd provide a home for numerous rare species of plant and animal. For human visitors the Mynd offers plenty of little-used paths and views across miles of countryside.

Here you will find bog pimpernel and spotted orchid, butterwort and bilberry. Among the birds are stonechat and ouzel, buzzard and even a few red grouse.

Along the top of the Mynd you can follow the Portway Track, an ancient drover's road, or explore 30 miles (48km) of footpaths.

WENLOCK EDGE

Near Church Stretton, Shropshire

Shropshire was one of just two English counties recently listed by the Council for the Protection of Rural England (CPRE) as having 'real' countryside – areas of countryside that are at least a mile or so from the nearest habitation or road. When you visit Wenlock Edge it is easy to see why the CPRE selected Shropshire.

the old workings can be seen everywhere.

Wenlock Edge is most valued now for its rare plants and animals. Tree species include wych elm, maple, ash and hazel. Among a host of rare limestone-loving plants are the wonderfully named splurge laurel, nettle-leafed bellflower and yellow archangel. Badgers, foxes and deer roam on the ground, while buzzards and kestrels swoop overhead. There is even a secluded Elizabethan manor house on the southern slopes, and if you are a member of the Youth Hostel Association you can stay there.

Best of all are the heavily overgrown tracks and paths, lined with unsprayed and untrimmed hedges. Here you will find tangled blackthorn and hazel, dogwood and elder, along walks unchanged since Housman's time.

This thin, 15-mile (24-km) limestone escarpment runs from Ironbridge – which takes its name from the world's oldest iron bridge, built by Abraham Darby in 1779 – to Craven Arms. The ridge is a mass of fossils, the bodies of millions of long-dead sea creatures, and was once a coral reef lapped by ocean waves. Tectonic plate movements over millions of years pushed up the ancient sea-bed to create the ridge we see today.

Like the Long Mynd (see page 111), Wenlock is associated with that great poet of the Shropshire countryside, A.E. Housman (1859–1936). In addition to the beauty of the landscape celebrated by Housman, there is a vast treasure of industrial archaeology in this important Site of Special Scientific Interest. Lime was quarried throughout the area from earliest times and limekilns – in which limestone was burned to produce fertilizer – were constructed from the Middle Ages onwards. The ancient woods were coppiced for centuries to provide fuel for the limekilns and traces of

RED HOUSE
GLASS CONE
Wordsley, West Midlands

For more than four centuries glass has been made in this corner of the Midlands.

The Red House Glass Cone was built in 1790 and continued to be used, amazingly, until as late as 1936. The cone soars to 100 feet (30 metres) high and is basically a furnace round which the glassmakers and blowers once carried on their trade. Four glass cones remain in the country, but this is the best example as it has hardly been altered since it was first built.

A spiral staircase leads visitors up through the cone to a viewing platform from which the extra-ordinary structure can be fully appreciated. Tunnels and passageways have only recently been opened to the public and, fascinatingly, the cone is still employed by glassmakers who demonstrate the skills that kept the business going for 200 years. There is also a splendid collection of glass that spans more than a century.

BOURNVILLE

Birmingham, West Midlands

Nowhere in the country is the Quakers' long history of practical good works and benevolence more evident than in this Birmingham suburb.

It was in 1879 that the Cadbury brothers, George and Richard, opened their famous chocolate factory.

Unlike most other industrialists of the time, they neither paid their workers the absolute minimum nor built houses for them that were unsanitary hovels. Instead they developed Bournville, an extraordinary model village where the architects were asked to build houses that had the look and feel of 'olde England'.

It was an admirable attempt to create a kind of idyllic English past – a past that never really existed, admittedly – and was a groundbreaking scheme. The brothers even went so far as to dismantle two genuine medieval houses and reassemble them in this suburban setting.

Each well-built cottage in Bournville was provided with a bathroom, which was almost unheard of in working-class housing at the time. The brothers made sure there was plenty of space for gardens and other open areas. Anyone who thinks that Victorian factory owners were all money-grasping ogres should visit this curious corner of south-west Birmingham and be prepared to have their opinions changed.

SOHO HOUSE

Handsworth, Birmingham, West Midlands

Classically beautiful Soho House comes as something of a surprise, located as it is just under 3 miles (5km) north of the architectural mishmash that is central Birmingham. The 18th-century house was the home of Matthew Boulton (1728–1809), a friend of the great scientist and engineer James Watt (1736–1819), and a key figure in the industrial development of Birmingham. The house has been beautifully restored to reflect the style of the 18th-century city, and it is easy to imagine Watt and Boulton in such splendid surroundings discussing the developments that caused Birmingham to become one of the great manufacturing centres of the world.

Boulton inherited his father's button-making business, but went on to produce objects in silver and gilded bronze at his Soho factory in Handsworth, which was then still in rural Staffordshire. His friendship with Watt led to the design and manufacture of steam engines, which were eventually exported all over the world. Boulton's other great claim to fame is that he set up the world's first steam-powered mint at Soho.

Soho House provides a rare glimpse into the private life of one of the 'fathers' of the Industrial Revolution.

Below: Soho House was the home of the industrialist Matthew Boulton (1728–1809). It was here that some of the greatest scientists of the 18th-century met, including the engineer James Watt (1736–1819) and Erasmus Darwin (1731–1802), grandfather of Charles.

CANNOCK CHASE

Near Cannock, Staffordshire

Above: Cannock Chase, with its rich areas of heath and woodland, survived despite the soot and grime of nearby mining and heavy industry.

The New Forest, Salisbury Plain, Dartmoor and Exmoor are well known right across the country, but Staffordshire's greatest area of open space, Cannock Chase – which is an officially designated Area of Outstanding Natural Beauty – is often overlooked by visitors to Britain.

Surrounded by old mining towns, such as Brereton, Norton Canes and Hednesford, Cannock Chase is a high plateau, bordered to the north by the Trent Valley and to the south by the industrial West Midlands, with a unique mix of industrial heritage and rich natural history.

The origins of the Chase as a medieval hunting forest can still be glimpsed where ancient trees have

survived and particuarly around Hednesbury Hills, where a large area of ancient heathland has escaped both the plough and the improvers.

Henry VIII's minister William Paget (1505–63) was gifted Cannock Chase early in the 16th century. He would have overseen small-scale mining for the rich seams of coal that characterize the underlying geology, but it wasn't until the middle decades of the 19th century that mining grew exponentially. Canals and railways made the boom possible and by the early part of the 20th century 23,000 men were carrying 4 million tons of coal a year to the surface.

But amid the dust and dirt the Chase survived

relatively unscathed, and now provides – as it did for those hard-pressed miners – a haven of relief from the pressures of everyday life. Fallow and muntjac deer haunt the woodlands; kestrels and other birds of prey hover above the bluebell woods and heaths; and although the mines have now gone their legacy remains in the old miners' cottages of nearby towns.

GLADSTONE POTTERY MUSEUM
Longton, Staffordshire

In the late 18th and early 19th centuries, this part of the Midlands became known as 'The Potteries' on account of its growing number of pottery manufacturers. At the Gladstone Pottery Museum a small part of the old Potteries survives in almost pristine condition. The museum is a former pottery factory, and has been kept just as it was during the early days of an industry that put Staffordshire firmly on the world map.

Gladstone is truly the last of its kind, and here visitors can see how pottery was made – from raw clay to final pot – in the early part of the 19th century. Arranged round a crooked cobbled yard are the curious coal-fired, bottle-shaped, brick-built kilns – works of art in themselves – that once lay at the heart of all pottery manufacture. Manufacturing conditions in the potteries were harsh, with fierce heat and dust. Archive film of the last potters – men and women still worked here in the 1930s and 1940s – is regularly shown, and visitors are even encouraged to try throwing a pot themselves.

In addition to the usual run of jugs and plates, decorative tiles were made here, as well as everything from artificial flowers to lavatories. The delicate hand painting that gave early pottery its distinctive look is still carried on by a few remaining craftsmen.

So if you want to discover exactly what a 'jollier', a 'jigger' and a 'saggermaker' once did, Gladstone is one of the few places in the world where you can still find out!

Left: To see how pottery was made during the early days of the Industrial Revolution visit Gladstone Pottery Museum, where jiggers and jolliers are still at work.

Opposite: Flint was once vital to pottery-making, and the Cheddleton Flint Mill shows how the stone was processed before being sent by canal to the great factories of Wedgwood and Spode.

CHEDDLETON FLINT MILL

Cheddleton, Staffordshire

The vast industrial output of the Midland potteries during the 19th century was fuelled, in part, by many long-forgotten chemical processes. Few traces of these remain today, but at least one has its memorial: the Cheddleton Flint Mill. The only mill of its kind surviving, Cheddleton reveals a fascinating trade without which Staffordshire's world-famous potteries could not have existed.

Cheddleton is a watermill at which flint was ground into powder, using water from the River Churnet to power the extraordinary mechanism still on view today. The raw flint was brought to Cheddleton by boat from Kent, and was then loaded into kilns and burned for several days to assist the grinding process.

The finely ground powder was sent via the nearby Cauldon Canal to the great pottery-making factories, such as Wedgwood and Spode. It was mixed with clay to add vital strength to the millions of jugs, cups, mugs, plates and ornamental ware produced and exported all over the world.

Today the complex consists of two watermills, a drying kiln, two burning kilns and the miller's cottage. The earliest parts of the South Mill date back to the 13th century when corn was probably ground here. Most of what we see today dates back to the 18th century and the beginning of the Industrial Revolution.

You can also visit nearby Cheddleton Station with its preserved steam railway. The station was the work of the great Victorian architect Augustus Pugin (1812–52), who also designed the Houses of Parliament.

THE SALT MUSEUM

Northwich, Cheshire

Britain's coal-mining industry is world-famous, but what of salt mining? This little-known industry was and is the preserve of Cheshire; even today Cheshire is the only place in the country where salt is commercially mined.

The value of salt in earlier times can be judged by the fact that the word 'salary' has the same Latin derivation as 'salt'. Salt was once a commodity of enormous value; it was taxed heavily at various times (£30 a ton in 1905), traded across Europe, and even used as a means of payment. The Salt Museum, housed in what was once the Northwich workhouse, keeps the history of the Cheshire salt-mining industry alive and gives the details of how it was extracted from deep beneath the Cheshire landscape, and by whom.

The vast salt deposits were laid down some 200 million years ago and have been mined since at least Roman times. The museum has an extraordinary collection of archive photographs dating back to the late 1860s showing the salt miners, their tools and the conditions under which they worked. Tools and artefacts involved in the trade are on permanent exhibition, together with models showing how the mines were operated.

Below: Alderley Edge, a patchwork of rare heathland and traditional woodland, looks out across the Cheshire Plain.

Shafts were dug to reach the 98-foot-thick (30-metre) bands of salt lying some 120 feet (37 metres) beneath the Northwich countryside. As the pillars of salt were dissolved by flooding in the shafts, the overlying rock collapsed, so explaining the massive amount of subsidence that can be seen in the surrounding area today.

ALDERLEY EDGE
Near Macclesfield, Cheshire

This is a fascinating area, rich in wildlife and with an extraordinary geology. The edge itself is a wooded sandstone escarpment, from the top of which are the best views in the county across the whole of the Cheshire Plain. The area west of the ancient wooded slope is old pasture mixed with stands of trees and now nationally rare areas of heathland. These provide a home for numerous threatened species of moth and butterfly, which thrive on the heather and bilberry that predominate on this unspoiled landscape.

There are ancient oaks as well as, to the west, beech, ash and pine. Throughout the area deer, fox and badger can be found, as well as numerous woodland bird species: woodpecker, tawny owl and redpoll, among others.

As with much of Cheshire, the underlying geology here is a fascinating maze of mineshafts and tunnels. Lead and copper were mined at Alderley from the Bronze Age onwards, and much of the deep network probably remains to be discovered. The numerous caves are regularly explored by local caving clubs, and the nearby Wizard Inn in Alderly Edge commemorates a legend about Merlin guarding the entrance to one of the caves.

BUXTON OPERA HOUSE
Buxton, Derbyshire

When people think of opera, the great metropolitan centres – London, Milan, Sydney – spring to mind. But, hidden away in a glorious part of Derbyshire on the edge of the Peak District is an opera house that can stand comparison with the best in the world.

Above: Buxton Opera House is grand and imposing. It is almost as if a small part of some great city has been brought to this pretty Peak District spa town.

A classic piece of Edwardian architecture, Buxton Opera House was lucky to survive the long period during the 1960s and 1970s when Britain became obsessed with television and home entertainment. But survive it did, despite being used as a cinema for some years, and it has recently been restored to its original Edwardian splendour.

Buxton Opera House has attracted some of the greatest names in entertainment history: Anna Pavlova performed here in 1935, and Gracie Fields and Hermione Gingold were regulars. Frank Matcham, an architect who specialized in music halls and theatres, designed the opera house and it was built in 1903. Matcham's most famous buildings, apart from Buxton, are the London Coliseum and the Hackney Empire, which is one of the last remaining old music halls.

The Buxton Opera Festival, which is based around the opera house, is held annually and visitors are invariably astonished at the beauty of their surroundings: the opera house is set in 25 acres (10 hectares) of ornamental gardens in the centre of this lovely old spa town.

MAM TOR – THE 'SHIVERING MOUNTAIN'
Hope Valley, Derbyshire

Few natural phenomena can compare with Mam Tor, which is in essence an extremely unstable mountain – so unstable that it has caused the permanent closure of the nearby A625 road, despite the best efforts of modern engineering.

Mam Tor is composed of extremely unstable horizontal layers of shale and gritstone. These materials are particularly prone to water damage: heavy annual rainfall seeps between the layers, freezes, expands, causes movement and adds to the general problem. The shale and gritstone continually crumble, and the mountain, in certain conditions, seems to shiver as it moves and decays.

Despite this seeming fragility, it is still safe to climb to the top of the tor where there is some evidence of an

Below: The Shivering Mountain really does 'shiver': horizontal layers of shale and gritstone are extremely unstable and prone to water damage, causing continual movement.

Iron Age hill fort. The climb is well worth it for the views along the Hope Valley and for the sense that you have climbed a mountain that is constantly on the move!

SPEEDWELL CAVERN
Near Castleton, Derbyshire

A narrow entrance leads to the top of more than 100 steps which descend from Winnats Pass – high up in the remote Peak District – to an incredible underground world that nothing above ground could ever have prepared you for.

At the bottom of the steps is a mysterious subterranean canal, which was dug by hand more than 200 years ago by lead miners. From here visitors can take a boat through this dripping, echoing, underground world. The canal runs eerily through seemingly endless tunnels, which are abandoned mine workings, before suddenly entering a vast system of natural caverns, lakes and rivers, hundreds of feet beneath the hills.

But the best is yet to come: at last the boat reaches the incredible Bottomless Pit, a huge underground lake

lying beneath a magnificent cavern roof. Even St Paul's pales into insignificance next to this extra-ordinary natural cathedral.

EYAM
Derbyshire

Eyam village is well known to students of social history, but deserves to be better known generally, if only because it gives history a human face. For the story of Eyam is not one of kings and queens, or even of the aristocracy. It's a tale of ordinary country people who had to face one of the most dreadful diseases in history: bubonic plague, commonly known as the Black Death.

The village sits just below Eyam Moor in the Derwent Valley, and has a Norman church and many old houses. In the High Street is Eyam Hall, which dates from 1676 and is still home to the Wright family, who built it. Their ancestors may well have lived and died through the plague that visited the village in the middle decades of the 17th century.

Eyam was also home to the Talbot and Hancock families in the 17th century. Their graves – known as Riley Graves from 'roylee', the name for a plot of land – lie just outside the village. The Hancocks lived in a house near the graves, of which nothing now remains. All we know is gleaned from the written record: Elizabeth Hancock cared for and buried her six children and her husband as each fell victim to the plague. It was only then that she abandoned the house. A similar fate overtook the Talbots and many other families in Eyam.

The real tragedy here is that once the disease was known to be among the villagers, they volunteered to stay put and cut themselves off from the rest of the world. They were unlucky because fleas carrying the plague – a common enough feature of city life, but which rarely reached remote rural settlements – were almost certainly brought to Eyam from London in a package of fabric in 1665, the year in which the capital was devastated by a similar outbreak.

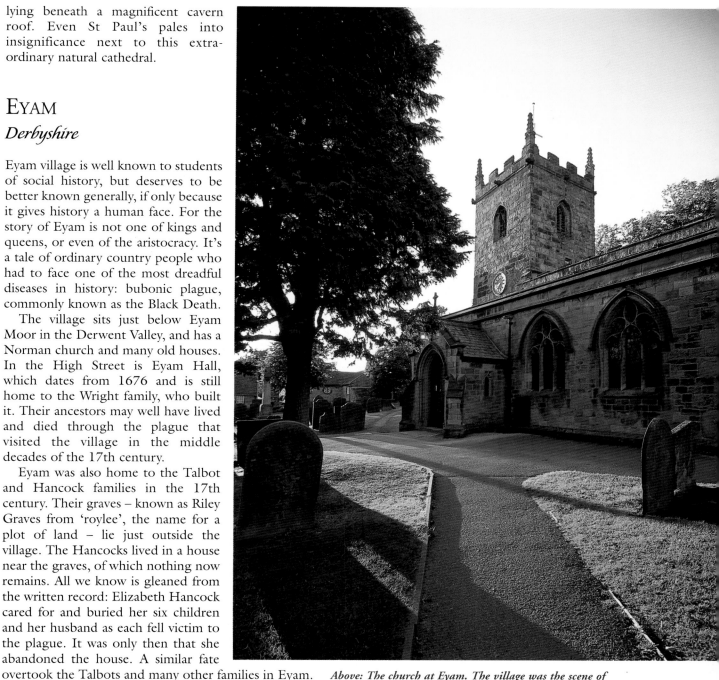

Above: The church at Eyam. The village was the scene of tragedy and heroism in the 17th century when it was visited by the Black Death. Eyam also boasts one of the most haunted buildings in England – the Miners Arms, where drink has been served since 1630.

The Miners Arms, in the main village, was where the Barmote Court once met to settle disputes between the local lead miners. It was built in 1630 and is said to be one of the most haunted buildings in England.

CALKE ABBEY
Ticknall, Derbyshire

Most National Trust houses have a well-kept, beautifully restored look, but in recent years there have been moves towards trying to show houses – be they stately homes or smaller buildings – more as they might have been at the time they were inhabited. Calke Abbey, tucked away in a quiet part of south Derbyshire, is a classic example of the 'lived-in' look.

Occupying the site of a former monastery (hence its name), the second biggest house in Derbyshire started its domestic life as a Tudor house, but like so many big country houses was updated in the 18th century. What makes Calke Abbey unique is the extraordinary family that owned it over the centuries.

The Harpurs made their fortune as lawyers in the late 16th century, but subsequent generations were notoriously reclusive. Visitors to the house were discouraged and today's photographers from glossy magazines would have been viewed as being beyond contempt. Generation after generation inherited the house and parklands and stayed put, living quietly at home. Over the years they collected a vast amount of furniture, books, pictures, toys, carriages, wall hangings and collections of stuffed birds and eggs. Nothing was ever thrown away. Eventually this huge collection filled the main rooms, storerooms, cupboards, corridors and even the attic.

When the National Trust acquired the house from Sir Henry, the last of the Harpurs, in 1985 they found an interior unchanged since the 1880s, that high Victorian period when drawing rooms were packed with pictures and ornaments and bric-à-brac. In some rooms the clutter is almost overwhelming, but with its slightly flaky plaster, dust and rickety furniture, its crowded passages and stairways, its clocks and ornaments, the house looks as if the family simply left it to its own devices. Perhaps most eccentric of all is the huge collection of natural-history specimens, the product of a lifetime's work of one Victorian incumbent, Sir Vauncey Harpur-Crewe.

When the Trust began to catalogue the items in the house they also found, still in its packing case, a complete and magnificent 18th-century state bed. Uniquely, because it had always been kept under wraps, none of the gorgeous hangings for the bed had ever been exposed to the light, so had not faded. It provides a glimpse – more authentic than most – into a vanished world.

Left: The first owners of Calke Abbey, the Harpur family, made their money as lawyers in the late 16th century, whereas later generations preferred to focus their energies on building up collections of anything and everything, from toys to carriages.

CUMBRIA, LANCASHIRE, YORKSHIRE & NORTHUMBERLAND

Once untamed and lawless, these wild upland counties still retain a fierce independence and in many ways have changed little over the centuries, hence the continued existence of so many unspoiled places.

KEY
1. Printing House Museum
2. Eskdale Watermill
3. Duddon Valley
4. Heysham Head
5. Hall-i'-th'-Wood
6. Barton Swing Aqueduct
7. Piece Hall
8. Saltaire
9. Bridestones Moor
10. Stephenson's Cottage
11. Allen Banks
12. Beadnell Limekilns
13. Bamburgh Castle and Beaches

PRINTING HOUSE MUSEUM
Cockermouth, Cumbria

Cockermouth is probably best known as the birthplace of the great Romantic poet William Wordsworth, but the little Cumbrian town is also home to a remarkable museum of printing.

The museum – which was the brainchild of a local printing enthusiast – is exceptionally well planned and laid out. It takes the visitor through the history of printing, from its invention in Europe in the 15th century, through 17th- and 18th-century innovations, the skills of Victorian and 20th-century typesetters, right up to modern computer printing.

Historic equipment from all over the world is on show, and visitors get the chance to try their hand at typesetting, which is not as easy as it looks! When you've set your page you can have it printed – or 'proofed', to use printers' jargon – on a hand press.

ESKDALE WATERMILL
Boot, Lake District, Cumbria

Eskdale is one of the loveliest valleys in the Lake District, and at its head stands one of the last remaining cornmills in the north of England. Dating from 1878, the mill retains its complete original timber workings. Documentary evidence suggests that milling has actually been carried out on this site since a few years after William the Conqueror's great Domesday survey.

Right: The Printing House Museum houses what is thought to be the biggest collection of early printing machinery in Britain, and visitors get the chance to try their hand at typesetting.

Remarkably, the mill was still grinding corn in this remote area of the country until well into the 20th century. Much of the gearing was kept when a dynamo was installed, and the waterwheel continued to be used right up to the mid-1950s to generate electricity. The mill then lay quiet until the 1970s, when its importance was recognized, and it was bought by the local council and fully restored.

A permanent exhibition details the history of the mill and how it works, and visitors can see corn being ground as it was for centuries, until modern techniques rendered watermills and windmills obsolete.

All around is the incomparable scenery of Eskdale, and you can even reach the mill just as in earlier times – via an ancient packhorse bridge over Whillan Beck in the splendidly named village of Boot.

DUDDON VALLEY
Lake District, Cumbria

The Duddon River runs for just over 17 miles (27km) from the Wrynose Pass to the estuary at Broughton-in-Furness, but what this little river valley lacks in length and size it more than makes up for in scenic quality. The Duddon Valley, with its woodlands, fells and tumbling streams, is one of the Lake District's hidden gems. There is just one village along the valley – the delightful hamlet of Ulpha – which may explain the slightly forgotten feel of the valley's wooded slopes.

Near the source of the river at Wrynose Pass there is the beautiful and ancient Birks packhorse bridge. From here you can look down into the dark waters that provide a home for numerous native brown trout. Tiny lanes wind along the valley, sometimes hugging the river, other times meandering away from it, and all along the route there is much to enjoy.

Near the source of the river, Hardknott Pass with its nearby Roman fort should not be missed, and further downstream, west of Broughton-in-Furness, is the ancient stone circle at Swineside.

Left: One of the Lake District's hidden gems, the Duddon Valley is a mix of woodlands, fells and tumbling crystalline streams.

HEYSHAM HEAD

Near Morecambe, Lancashire

Cliffs of red Triassic sandstone at the seaward end of this wonderful headland provide glorious views across Morecambe Bay and the Lake District beyond. Mostly heathland, with some woodland, Heysham also has much of archaeological interest, including the remains of spectacular rock-cut graves and the 8th-century St Patrick's Chapel (a scheduled ancient monument), named after the legend of St Patrick, who is said to have survived a shipwreck on the coast here.

In spring you'll see carpets of bluebells across the headland where the bracken and bramble, grassland and low shrub cover allow. The areas of woodland support oak and elm, ash and – rather too plentiful for some – sycamore.

Heysham's cliffs are also home to the sea spleenwort, a rare fern, not found elsewhere in this part of the country.

HALL-I'-TH'-WOOD

Near Bolton, Lancashire

Just to the north-east of Bolton can be found one of Britain's most remarkable ancient timber-framed houses. Set in the town of Tongue (probably from the Old Norse 'tangi' or Old English 'tang', meaning 'a narrow strip of land'), Hall-i'-th'-Wood was built from timber cut from the ancient oak woodland that once covered this whole area. The name of the old house suggests that it was once deep within that very woodland that was inhabited by wild boar, deer and more.

The house was built in the early part of the 16th century, and probably completed in 1530, by a wealthy local landowner called Lawrence Brownlow, who chose

Below: Hall-i'-th'-Wood is a testament to the pride and wealth of a medieval landowner: the house is exuberantly decorated with far more timber than its structure requires.

a high, easily defended position above Eagley Brook. The house was extended at the end of the 16th century and then again in the 1640s.

By 1758 it was being rented out to the family of one Samuel Crompton (1753–1827), a remarkable man. As a child, Crompton watched his mother spinning yarn in one of the upstairs rooms at the hall, and began to experiment in new ways of increasing the speed and efficiency of weaving. Before Crompton was 30 years old he had invented the 'mule' – the first multiple-spindle machine able to produce top-quality yarn.

During the 19th century, the stone-and-timber house fell into disrepair until it was rescued and restored by Lord Leverhulme in 1900. It is now a fascinating museum. Visitors can wander through 10 rooms of the house and view a collection of early furniture and objects associated with Samuel Crompton and his spinning machine.

BARTON SWING AQUEDUCT

Barton-upon-Irwell
Greater Manchester

There is nothing in the world quite like the Barton Swing Aqueduct, which was built in 1893 to carry the Bridgwater Canal across the Manchester Ship Canal. This extraordinary piece of engineering is a testimony to the Victorian engineers' belief in progress, reflecting their conviction that industry and effort could overcome any obstacle.

The original stone aqueduct on the site was too low over the Manchester Ship Canal for anything other than relatively small vessels to pass under it. The swing aqueduct solved the problem. Now, when bigger boats need to use the Manchester Ship Canal, the swing aqueduct can be turned until it is at right angles to the Bridgwater Canal (which it normally carries), thus allowing boats of up to 20,000 tons through.

Left: Victorian engineers believed that no obstacle was too great to be surmounted, hence the extraordinary undertaking that is the Barton Swing Aqueduct.

The aqueduct has massive gates at either end to trap the water in the canal while it is being moved out of alignment, is more than 230 feet (70 metres) long and holds more than 800 tons of water. That weight, added to the huge weight of the aqueduct itself – another 800 tons – adequately explains why the aqueduct is justly considered one of the wonders of the industrial world.

PIECE HALL
Halifax, West Yorkshire

As recently as the 1970s, the Piece Hall in Halifax, the last of England's great 18th-century north-country cloth markets, was in danger of demolition. Even when the hall was restored in 1976, the 300 small shops inside were hacked about to allow modern commercial businesses in – but at least the hall survives.

It is an extraordinary building. Built in stone to a wonderful classical design – two storeys above an arcaded ground floor – and organized around a large

Above: Like some great classical piazza, Halifax's Piece Hall – completed in 1779 – once brought together 300 small shopkeepers and tradesmen.

cobbled square, the Piece Hall was once the centre of the commercial world of hand-loom weavers from villages and isolated cottages all over this part of Yorkshire, for this is where they sold their wares.

The hall opened in 1779, but by the middle decades of the 19th century hand-loom weaving had been all but obliterated by huge mechanized weaving mills. The Piece Hall struggled on, and by the late 19th century it was a wholesale market. In 1928, it was officially recognized as an ancient monument, but even that designation did nothing to secure its future, and on several occasions it nearly went the way of the cloth halls of Leeds, Bradford and Wakefield, all of which have been demolished.

The Piece Hall fell into disrepair, but the basic structure remained sound until restoration finally took place in 1972. Today it is home to a wide range of shops and cafés, restaurants and other businesses.

One curious legend about the Piece Hall concerns handprints that were once visible on the exterior wall near Westgate. It is said that more than a century and a half ago a murderer trying to escape his pursuers found the gate to the hall closed, and fleetingly touched the wall with both hands before rushing off in another direction. The soot-blackened walls retained the white image of the murderer's hands until the 1976 restoration cleaned the stone and removed all trace of the prints.

SALTAIRE
Near Shipley, West Yorkshire

Just to the north of Bradford, deep in that part of Yorkshire inextricably linked with the famous literary family, the Brontës, is the village of Saltaire. Saltaire was purpose-built in the 19th century to provide decent accommodation for factory workers in the local woollen mills, at a time when most factory owners allowed their employees to live in conditions of the utmost poverty and degradation.

The village was built as a 'model' or ideal village by the great woollen-mill owner Sir Titus Salt (1803–76), one of the most remarkable figures in that great period of industrial expansion that made Britain the commercial centre of the world.

Saltaire is such a remarkable place that it has been designated a World Heritage Site by UNESCO, along with such historic sites as Stonehenge and the Roman city of Bath.

The houses and shops are simple, brick-built and by no means grand, but compared to the Victorian slums of Manchester and Leeds, Saltaire must have seemed like heaven to industrial workers in the 19th century. The streets are broad enough to give the village a light, almost open feel, and the houses have good-sized windows and are solidly built.

Unlike those pious mill and factory

Left: With their many windows and elegant construction, the mills at Saltaire would have been filled with light to create an appealing working environment, and they were a unique response to the general inhumanity of early industrial buildings.

owners who went devoutly to church each Sunday but were happy at the same time to work their staff to death, Sir Titus Salt was both a businessman and a genuine, practical philanthropist. He deserves to be remembered, and Saltaire is his monument.

BRIDESTONES MOOR
Near Whitby, North Yorkshire

The strange sandstone stacks rising up from this lonely moor in the wilds of North Yorkshire were laid down as sediment at the bottom of the sea during the Jurassic period some 206 to 144 million years ago. Later earth movements forced them into their present position, and erosion over the succeeding millennia has produced the strange outcrops we see today. The stacks stare down on a rare heathland habitat of heather mixed with numerous sedges and other plants, such as bilberry and crowberry.

Linked to Blakey Topping and Crosscliff, the moor is a Site of Special Scientific Interest, managed by the National Trust. Many rare plants grow in cracks in the rocks here, including wall rue and maidenhair. At Dovedale Wood – one of the oldest areas of woodland in the country – there are ancient oaks mixed with thick, luscious areas of fern and honeysuckle, moss and lichen. A 1½-mile (2.4-km) nature trail runs through these varied habitats.

Blakey Topping is one of the strangest parts of this remote and beautiful region: from the distance it rises up, cone-shaped and heather-clad, from a vast sea of green forest. The view from the top is one of the best-kept secrets of this part of Yorkshire.

Below: Wide and windswept, Bridestones Moor is home to numerous rare plants, including bilberry and crowberry.

Stephenson's Cottage

Near Wylam, Northumberland

The Industrial Revolution might not have been quite as world-changing as it eventually was without the inventions of George Stephenson (1781–1848), yet the origins of this extraordinary man were very humble. Visitors to his isolated cottage will find it hard to believe that the little boy who was born here in 1781 was destined to take the world by storm and – via the steam engine – change the nature and pace of transport forever.

Above: George Stephenson (1781–1848), one of the greatest figures of the Industrial Revolution, was born in this tiny, remote cottage on the banks of the River Tyne.

Stephenson's *Rocket* launched the era of railway travel when, in September 1825, it ran from Darlington to Stockton carrying 450 people at the then staggering speed of 15 miles (25km) an hour.

The Stephenson family, who were poor if not destitute, would at least have enjoyed clean air and water as the house overlooked the River Tyne. Before long, however, the Tyne became so dirty that few, if

Right: It took 30 years to create the extraordinary gardens at Allen Banks. Steps, paths and bridges – such as this one over the River Allen – guide the visitor through a wonderland of plants and trees.

any, salmon were able to penetrate as far as Wylam, let alone reach their spawning beds further upstream. Happily, the huge clean-up that accompanied the disappearance of the last of the traditional industries of the north-east means that salmon now lie regularly beneath Wylam Bridge, just as they would have done when Stephenson was born.

To reach the birthplace of the Father of the Railways you have to walk half a mile from Wylam Bridge, a pretty, largely stone-built village that straddles the River Tyne about 12½ miles (20km) inland from Newcastle upon Tyne, along the track that the great man would once have followed.

Allen Banks
Bardon Mill, Northumberland

Scenic views, a beautiful woodland garden, mature trees and an idyllic pond together make up one of the north-east's best-kept secrets. The gardens here were lovingly created by Susan Davidson, wife of the local landowner, between 1830 and 1860, using stone steps and paths to guide the visitor through a series of delightful vistas on the 200-acre (81-hectare) site on the banks of the River Allen.

When you cross the suspension bridge over the steep ravine above the river, keep a look out for dippers and wagtails. Then head south to Staward Wood, where there is a medieval tower house and gateway. Tower houses were once typical of this area, for Northumberland remained a lawless place until well into the 18th century. The border rievers (raiders) were continually feuding, and they organized cattle raids and revenge attacks back and forth across the border with Scotland. The authorities could do little to police these remote uplands, which is why fortified houses remained the norm long after they had ceased to be built elsewhere in the country.

Staward Wood is said to be very ancient. Certainly it is rich in rare plants, including the wood fescue and moschatel, and it is one of the red squirrel's last strongholds in England.

Below: The quiet village of Beadnell was once a hive of industrial activity, but now only the shells of the old limekilns remain. Lime was burned in the kilns to provide fertilizer for the fields of eastern and southern England.

BEADNELL LIMEKILNS
Beadnell, Northumberland

If average annual temperatures in Northumberland were a little higher, the county's fabulous sandy beaches would be the talk of Europe. But the cold winds that slice in across the North Sea keep the beautiful, seemingly endless stretches of sand uncluttered. Overlooked by the ghostly remains of numerous castles and ancient fishing villages, the Northumbrian coast – and indeed the whole of the county – is one of the least visited places in England.

But among all the lovely villages of this windswept coast, Beadnell is one of the most interesting. Despite being close to the main Great North Road that links Newcastle to Edinburgh, this is a quiet place with a slightly forgotten air. However, the village's harbour walls and massive limekilns were built in the 18th century, when it was a bustling industrial centre. The massive kilns were fed daily with limestone mined from a large quarry to the south of the village. Once the lime had been burned it was loaded onto ships and carried south to fertilize the fields of Lincolnshire, Kent, East Anglia and Sussex.

Before the advent of modern fertilizers, lime was a staple of agricultural success, and it put Beadnell on the map. The lime-burning process was relatively straightforward. Fresh lime was poured into the top of the kiln with plenty of coal (five parts lime to one part coal), and the kiln was fired to around 1832°F (1000°C) before being allowed to cool slowly. The valuable cooked lime was then removed from the base of the kiln.

Beadnell is one of the last places in the country that could be described as a lime-burning village: the limekilns operated from the mid-1700s until 1858, and in that time the village's population grew from a few dozen to more than 500.

BAMBURGH CASTLE AND BEACHES

Bamburgh, Northumberland

Above: Despite numerous periods of restoration, Bamburgh Castle retains a forbidding medieval air from where it sits atop a rocky promontory.

From the entrance to the internationally important bird sanctuary at Budle Bay, south to the great fortress castle of Bamburgh, stretch the wide sands of one of Northumberland's best beaches. The walk will take you little more than an hour, but it is worth it, as these beaches are never crowded and afford breathtaking views over wide, unspoiled country.

Bamburgh itself is a pretty sandstone village, famous as the birthplace of the early Victorian heroine Grace Darling. One dreadful stormy night in 1838 Grace, aged just 23, rowed out with her father to help save the crew of a boat wrecked on the Farne Islands. Overnight she became nationally renowned. Sadly, she died young of consumption, but not before Queen Victoria had insisted on meeting her. A small museum – complete with replica rowing boat and items once owned by Grace – commemorates her life.

Brooding over the little village is Bamburgh Castle. Once a medieval fortress, it was converted into more comfortable domestic accommodation in the 18th century. High on its rocky precipice, it still seems to intimidate the humbler houses and cottages nestling below its walls.

Back on the beach you can walk south for many miles, enjoying some of the most bracing sea airs and cleanest sands in Europe.

WALES

Unspoiled medieval towns, hidden chapels and farms, magnificent gardens, windswept islands, ruined castles and remote uplands all contribute to the romantic character of this ancient kingdom.

KEY

1. Conwy
2. Newborough Beach
3. Portmeirion
4. Dinas Island
5. St Govan's Chapel
6. Aberglasney Gardens
7. Aberdeunant
8. Joseph Parry's Cottage
9. Castell Coch
10. The Kymin
11. The Begwns

Conwy

Conwy

Conwy is a remarkably well-preserved medieval town. Even today, centuries after they were first built, the sturdy town walls – almost 26 feet (8 metres) thick in places – still link a succession of substantial forts, each situated precisely 50 yards (45 metres) from the last and each a stronghold in its own right. Conwy would have been impregnable when Edward I (1239–1307) established his castle here, one of a series of fortifications that marked the then border between Wales and England. The line of massive castles was intended to subdue the Welsh, who were known to be fierce, independent and difficult to control.

There are 21 bastions, and visitors can walk right round the town atop the Conwy Wall, which rises quickly from the West Gate to its highest point at the tower on the north-west corner. From here you can look out across the estuary, or back across a town that looks much as medieval London might have done.

Above: Many medieval buildings survive in Britain, but almost complete medieval towns are rare. Conwy, with its castle and ancient bridge, is remarkable in this respect.

Fortunately, all 1400 yards (1280 metres) of Conwy's town walls, along with many of the old houses within, managed to escape the attentions of the notorious town planners and architects of the 1960s and 1970s.

Conwy Castle, a dark, forbidding sight even today, sits high above the town, on a knoll within the walls. The castle was built in the late 13th century by a mason brought in specially by the king from mainland Europe, but by 1620 it had fallen into a bad state of repair. It was bought in 1628 by Viscount Conwy, whose family lived here until the local council took over in the 19th century. Today the castle is looked after by CADW (Welsh Historic Monuments).

Among the most interesting buildings in the town is what is generally agreed to be the smallest house in Britain: a tiny one-up, one-down cottage, 10 feet (3 metres) high and less than 6 feet (2 metres) wide, with barely enough room to turn round inside. There is also

Plas Mawr, a magnificent Elizabethan merchant's house, with original and beautiful plaster ceilings still intact.

When you've explored the town, take a look at Thomas Telford's magnificent bridge over the River Conwy; its towers were designed to complement those of the medieval castle.

NEWBOROUGH BEACH

Newborough, Anglesey

Just 2 miles (3.2km) south of the village of Newborough on the island of Anglesey, and a stone's throw from the road, is a hidden beach of quite breathtaking beauty. Newborough Beach is one of the most spectacular places along this weather-worn coast. Walk for mile after mile along the pure white sand, and the hustle and bustle of everyday life will seem a million miles away. There are superb views towards Snowdonia and the Llŷn Peninsula. From the car park, turn left along the beach, and an hour's walking will bring you to the spectacular Menai Strait between Anglesey and the Welsh mainland. Retrace your steps and turn right, and the wide sands lead to Llanddwyn Island, a narrow strip of land cut off now and again by high tides.

The sand dune system behind the beach is Newborough Warren, a rich and varied National Nature Reserve. Among the species that come here to breed are Canada goose, teal and shelduck. Summer visitors include oystercatcher, ringed plover and lapwing, and there are healthy populations of kestrel and sparrow-hawk. Newborough Forest, the coniferous plantation behind the dunes, is rich in birdlife, including crossbills, and there are numerous footpaths through this remote and lovely mix of freshwater lake, mudflat and tidal inlet.

Llanddwyn Island has much to interest the historian. There are the remains of an early church as well as two lighthouses and a terrace of sailors' cottages. The church is dedicated to St Dwynwen, the patron saint of lovers; and when you gaze across this wildly romantic landscape that dedication seems utterly appropriate.

Below: Weather-worn and spectacular, the broad sands of Newborough Beach will take you from Llanddwyn Island all the way to Anglesey.

PORTMEIRION

Near Porthmadog, Gwynedd

Bright, quirky, charming, eccentric, delightful: over the years these and many similar words have been used to describe this extraordinary village on the Welsh coast. It would take an architectural historian to understand every stylistic twist and turn in a village that is essentially the life's work of one man: the architect Clough Williams-Ellis (1883–1978).

In many ways, Williams-Ellis was a man ahead of his time. He wanted to prove that man-made structures did not necessarily ruin a beautiful natural setting, so he spent 50 years (1925–75) building this village on the peninsula he owned. With its whitewashed and pastel-coloured cottages, Portmeirion resembles something from the Mediterranean, and achieves just what its architect intended. Surrounded by gardens and woodlands and miles of beautiful beach, it fits well into an Area of Outstanding Natural Beauty. Williams-Ellis was a passionate conservationist well before such ideas were fashionable, and he would be delighted to know that the village is now in the hands of a registered charity called The Second Portmeirion Foundation, which carefully guards his legacy.

The Portmeirion Hotel lets out the cottages in the village, and there are restaurants, shops and delightful walks. Williams-Ellis's creation was notably the setting for the cult 1960s BBC television series *The Prisoner*.

Above: The 1960s BBC television series The Prisoner *was filmed in Portmeirion, a village that became the life's work of its architect Clough Williams-Ellis.*

DINAS ISLAND

Near Fishguard, Pembrokeshire

The Pembrokeshire coast is one of those rare places where it is possible to feel a real sense of escape from the pressures of the world. Dinas Island (sometimes known as Dinas Head), 100 acres (40.5 hectares) of heath and bracken-covered grazing land, is a geological and archaeological treasure – and isn't actually an island at all. It's a headland that was once separated from the mainland by a deep, narrow channel cut by a glacier and then, over thousands of years, slowly filled with layers of peat. Archaeologists believe that there are the remains of an Iron Age hill fort, Pen Castell, on the headland.

Today, numerous paths and a circular coastal walk allow the visitor to explore the spectacular headland with its wonderful views across Cardigan Bay. The greatest pleasure of Dinas – apart from the views – is the fact that it is rarely visited and is home to important colonies of guillemots, fulmars and razorbills. On the seaward-facing bracken-covered slopes, there are colonies of small blue butterfly and thrift clearwing moth.

ST GOVAN'S CHAPEL
Near Bosherston, Pembrokeshire

Hidden away on the remote Pembrokeshire coast is St Govan's Chapel, a minuscule stone cell built in the 13th century which seems to cling to the rocky cliff face. It is difficult to imagine a more austere, unworldly spot.

No one quite knows who St Govan was, as he is not recorded in any early texts, but there is a theory that he may have been the Sir Gawain of Arthurian legend. According to one tale, St Govan, or Gawain, was pursued to this lonely rock face by invading Vikings. Timely intervention by the Holy Spirit – or some such supernatural agency – allowed the rock to open just enough to let St Govan in but keep his pursuers out.

Curious markings on the wall at the back of the chapel are said to show where St Govan's ribs brushed the wall as the rock opened to receive him.

Whatever the truth behind the chapel, it is certainly a remarkable place. Archaeological evidence suggests that it may replace a 6th-century or earlier building. To reach it you have to descend steep steps cut into the cliff face. It is said that some supernatural influence makes it impossible for anyone to count the steps, but the journey is well worth it if only for the spectacular views out across the sea. It also gives you the chance to wonder at the strength of the religious fervour that drove the early Christians to spend their lives in such isolated spots.

Close to the chapel – but sadly now filled in – is a well where pilgrims once came in sufficient numbers for the waters to gain a reputation for healing.

Opposite: Built from stone and virtually inaccessible, the tiny chapel of St Govan has perched precariously on the side of a Pembrokeshire cliff since the 13th century.

ABERGLASNEY GARDENS
Llangathen, Carmarthenshire

One of Wales's best-kept secrets, this beautiful house has a rather chequered past. Largely rebuilt early in the 18th century, it is said to have 15th-century origins, but there is no firm evidence for this date. The house sits quietly in the lovely Tywi Valley and is currently undergoing restoration following decades of neglect.

The real treasure at Aberglasney, however, is the garden. The yew tunnel – a row of ancient yews carefully nurtured so that they now form a long arch – is almost certainly unique in Britain. It is said that the trees were planted when the house was rebuilt over two centuries ago, but they are almost certainly far older.

The Courtyard Garden is also a remarkable survivor. The house forms one side of the courtyard, while on the other three sides a walkway is supported on a series of stone arches. The formal gardens would have been viewed from this vantage point. Almost every example of this type of raised-walkway courtyard garden vanished in the 18th century with changing fashions in garden design, particularly with the growing passion

Below: The Cloister Garden is enclosed on three sides by a raised walkway, from which all of Aberglasney's formal gardens can be viewed.

for sweeping landscapes à la Capability Brown. Aberglasney, being remote from centres of fashion, kept its old-style garden, which was rediscovered under dense vegetation in the 1990s.

The Pool Garden is said to contain the valuable wine collection of a Victorian inhabitant of the house. The collection was inherited by a new teetotal owner in around 1900, and he was so outraged by the number of bottles in the cellar that he promptly threw them all in the lake, where it is believed they remain to this day. Occasional dredging has indeed turned up a few bottles.

The Stream Garden is a huge contrast to the more formal gardens nearer the house: here, moisture-loving plants have been introduced round the pond, surrounded by mature deciduous trees.

ABERDEUNANT

Near Llandeilo, Carmarthenshire

History comes alive when we see how people really lived in the past – not through court rolls or other official documents, but through their houses, the implements they used, the food they ate and the clothes they wore.

Above: The farmland of Aberdeunant Estate has never been intensively cultivated, so its fields and meadows are particularly rich in wild flowers.

The old farmhouse at Aberdeunant is one of the few places in Wales where it is possible to glimpse agricultural life as it was before 20th-century mechanization swept away a thousand years of farming history.

The house is delightful and rare, partly because it is so tiny; only the *gegin fawr* (large kitchen) is open to the public. It is incomparably picturesque, and has always been a working farm. The house is cruck framed – a structure that reveals its medieval origins – and may well have started life as a simple hall, a style of building that would have been familiar in Saxon times.

In the farmyard, evidence of the way in which this remote farm developed over the centuries is clear: the barn, tool shed and stable date variously from the late 17th century through to the 19th century. Built of local stone they are all slate-roofed, although the farmhouse is still thatched.

One of the most remarkable things about Aberdeunant is that the land around it has never been intensively farmed. Its pastures and meadows have never been 'improved', sprayed or ploughed, so in spring and summer they are rich in wild flowers.

JOSEPH PARRY'S COTTAGE
Merthyr Tydfil, Mid Glamorgan

This small, unassuming house makes no claims to greatness on the grounds of its architectural splendour, nor because it was once the home of a powerful lord. But its very ordinariness is what makes it so special: it is a typical ironworker's house from the 1840s. Its survival is little short of miraculous, and can be attributed to the fact that Dr Joseph Parry, arguably Wales's best-known composer, was born here in 1841.

Parry moved to America with his family when he was just 13. His prodigious talents were recognized, and money was raised to send him eventually back to England and the Royal College of Music. He was a prolific composer whose work includes operas, songs and pieces for piano, but he is best known today for his hymns *Aberystwyth* and *Myfanwy*. In later life he became Professor of Music at University College, Cardiff, but like so many great Welshmen his origins were remarkably humble.

Today, the cottage where Parry was born looks just as it would have done when he was a boy. Furniture and decoration from the period combine with memorials to the composer to create a unique glimpse

Above: Great houses often survive the ravages of time, but the houses of working people are invariably changed out of all recognition or bulldozed. Joseph Parry's Cottage is a rare exception to that rule.

of life in Merthyr Tydfil more than a century and a half ago, when its industrial might made this one of the most important places in Wales.

In front of the cottage is a short preserved section of the Glamorganshire Canal which once linked Merthyr to the docks at Cardiff. A little further away in Blaenavon, and worth a visit, is Big Pit, where you can descend almost 305 feet (100 metres) to the coal face, taking the same journey underground that faced hundreds of miners every day of their working lives over the centuries when coal was the lifeblood of this area.

CASTELL COCH
Tongwynlais, Cardiff

The Victorians took the Gothic style to their hearts, and this love affair manifested itself in, among other things, the pre-Raphaelite painters' obsession with the idea of medieval and Arthurian chivalry. It was also reflected in an almost universal admiration among architects for the Gothic style. St Pancras Station in London is perhaps the most spectacular example, but up and down the country Gothic castles, houses, bridges and follies were built. Indeed, in at least one case – Castell Coch, near Cardiff – the desire for Gothic reached almost fairy-tale proportions.

Castell Coch – meaning 'red castle' after the stone from which it was built – is almost, but not entirely, a Victorian creation; it was built on the ruins of an 11th-century castle. Even the experts agree, however, that the general external appearance of the castle is, to a large extent, authentic – although the interior design is a decidedly fantastical idea of what constituted medieval Gothic.

It was the Marquis of Bute (1847–1900) who commissioned William Burges (1827–81) to build his castle which, with its three towers rising above the surrounding hills, is both gloriously romantic and militarily imposing. Bute, one of the world's richest men, wanted the castle to embody the very spirit of the medieval Gothic world, but he also wanted it to be a comfortable home. This was a tall order, but Burges was told to spare no expense in achieving Bute's dream home. Work started in 1875 and wasn't finished until 1891, 10 years after Burges himself had died.

For the visitor, you enter via a covered staircase that leads to the huge banqueting hall, whose roof of beautifully stencilled wooden panels rises above walls painted with magnificent scenes of the deaths of early Christian martyrs. The arcading is gorgeously painted, too, and above the fireplace is a splendid figure of St Lucius.

One end of the hall leads to the kitchen tower; the other takes us into the spectacularly decorated – some would say over-decorated – keep tower. Here, the octagonal drawing room has a two-storeyed ribbed dome both gilded and brightly painted. Every conceivable animal and plant seems to be depicted here, from foxes, monkeys and lizards to creatures from Greek mythology and Aesop's Fables.

Higher in the tower is Lady Bute's bedroom – again with a double-domed ceiling and painted with mythological creatures, animals and birds. Lord Bute's own bedroom, which has an ornately carved fireplace, is above the keep.

Despite all the time, effort and expense spent on his abode, there is no evidence that Lord Bute was particularly enthralled by his creation; he stayed in the castle only infrequently and died within a decade of its completion.

Opposite: The secluded entrance to the Kymin leads you into the wooded gardens that seductively hide the extraordinary Round House.

Left: Castell Coch is a Victorian fairy-tale creation, but in its detail it is an authentic-looking medieval castle.

THE KYMIN

Near Monmouth, Monmouthshire

The Wye Valley is not seen as a major tourist attraction, which is surprising given how beautiful and unspoilt it is. There are so many places along the valley deserving mention that it is difficult to make a selection, but one stands out: The Kymin. Situated high above the town of Monmouth, this beautiful wooded garden hides the Round House. Built as a banqueting house towards the end of the 18th century, the Round House provided a venue for the regular Tuesday lunch gatherings of Monmouth's gentlemen. Originally these were held in the open air, but a year after they began in 1794, a heavy downpour encouraged the gentlemen to build the house we see today. The Round House dining room could be hired for 1/6d., and from its five windows guests could enjoy views across 10 counties – weather permitting.

Such was the popularity of the Round House that the gardens were landscaped, walks and seats were built, a bowling green was installed and a telescope was provided on the roof 'for the pleasure of the more scientific among us'.

Close by is a monument to Admiral Lord Nelson and other admirals of the Fleet. It was built in 1801 and Nelson came to see it soon after. The National Trust has restored the Round House, which now looks much as it did when the gentlemen of Monmouth first came here to dine more than two centuries ago.

THE BEGWNS

Near Hay-on-Wye, Radnorshire

Snowdonia is probably the best known area of remote countryside in Wales, but there are other places just as special – such as the Begwn Hills. This remote and beautiful upland – nearly 1300 acres (527 hectares) in all – runs along the ridge of the hills on the extreme southern edge of the Radnorshire Commons, and is almost hemmed in by the wealth of valleys, towns and distant farms that surround it. There are unparalleled views far out across the Brecon Beacons and the Black Mountains.

The peaceful Begwns are also important from an archaeological point of view, as the whole of this upland common is a mass of ancient boundaries and enclosures. Habitation seems to have been particularly dense at the southern tip of the plateau, where archaeologists have discovered the remains of dozens of long-vanished houses, tracks and field boundaries – evidence almost certainly of an abandoned medieval village.

SCOTLAND

Every corner of this land of mountains, distilleries and catsles contains

some long-forgotten ruin, ancient tower, bizarre architectural folly,

ruined abbey or evidence of far earlier civilizations.

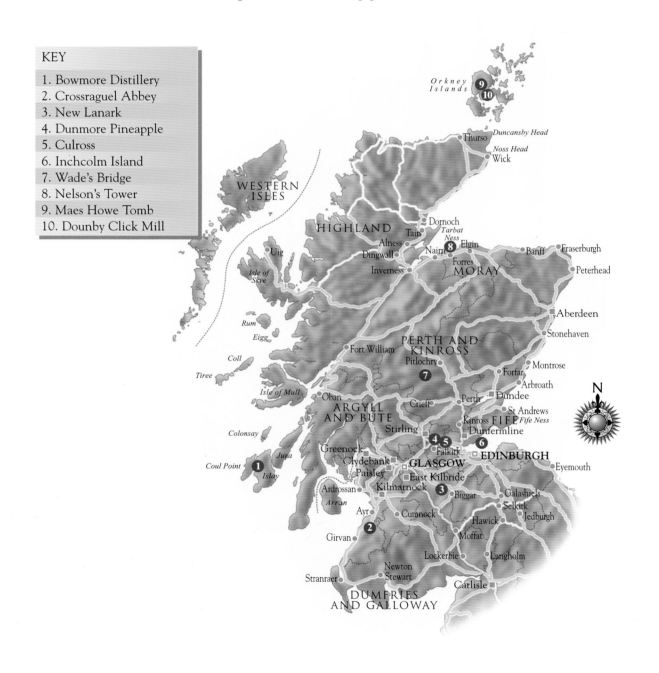

KEY

1. Bowmore Distillery
2. Crossraguel Abbey
3. New Lanark
4. Dunmore Pineapple
5. Culross
6. Inchcolm Island
7. Wade's Bridge
8. Nelson's Tower
9. Maes Howe Tomb
10. Dounby Click Mill

BOWMORE DISTILLERY

Isle of Islay, Argyll & Bute

Scotland has many distilleries; indeed, the country is famed for its whisky all over the world. One of its earliest and least modernized distilleries is found on the remote west-coast island of Islay.

Bowmore Distillery was built on the remote shores of Loch Indaal in 1779. It has had just five owners in more than two centuries and each one has continued to produce whisky using techniques identical to those followed in the earliest days.

With each passing year, fewer distilleries are able to continue the ancient traditions, but Bowmore has stayed true to its history and still employs a maltman, whose job it is to turn the barley on the malting floor using a specially designed wooden shovel.

The heart of every good whisky, of course, is the water from which it is made. Bowmore whisky draws from the River Laggan, whose peaty waters have been percolating through the rocky hills for 2000 years. It is a combination of the precise nature of the rocks, the richness of the peat and the location of Bowmore at the sea's edge that enables the distillery to produce a whisky that is highly sought after by connoisseurs all over the world.

Perhaps the most interesting parts of the distillery are the ancient vaults, which are pretty much unchanged since the distillery was built. The vaults are filled with giant oak barrels in which the whisky must mature for years before it is ready for sale.

Below: Oak casks of Bowmore's fine whisky, which is distilled using centuries-old techniques, spend some time maturing on the shores of Loch Indaal.

CROSSRAGUEL ABBEY

Maybole, Ayrshire

A surprisingly large amount of Crossraguel Abbey, which was extended over the centuries, still survives, despite the destruction carried out during the Reformation and later plunder for building materials. Its survival may have been thanks to its isolated position.

Today, the 15th-century choir building, with its beautiful carvings still in place, is open to the public, along with the gatehouse with its curious corner turret. Visitors can climb the stairs to enjoy the fine view over the abbey grounds and the glorious Ayrshire country-side beyond.

Below: Gaunt and castle-like, Crossraguel Abbey – with its curious corner tower – survived the worst destruction of the Reformation, perhaps because of its remote location.

The abbey was founded by the Cluniacs, a reformed Benedictine order that originated in Cluny, France in *c.* AD 900. The name 'Crossraguel' probably comes from the Gallic for 'cross of Riaghail'. Riaghail, or St Regulus, was a Greek monk who came to Scotland in the Dark Ages.

One terrifying, but also rather amusing, story about the abbey concerns the 16th-century Earl of Cassilis, who tried to exert his authority over the abbot by roasting him slowly over a fire until he agreed to sign over the lands and revenue!

NEW LANARK

South Lanarkshire

Despite its designation as a World Heritage Site, New Lanark – a complete industrial village which was purpose-built to provide houses for those who worked

in the local 18th-century cotton mill – is not as well known as it should be.

What makes New Lanark unique is that it is a monument to a remarkable man, the social reformer and industrialist Robert Owen (1771–1858), whose ideas and treatment of his workers were at least a century ahead of their time.

While most mill owners and managers allowed their workers to live in the utmost poverty, toiling for up to 16 hours a day, with dreadful sanitation, no health care and the poorest quality food, Owen set off down a different path. He built good houses, which still stand today, set up schools for the mill-workers' children, organized evening classes for adult workers, offered free health care and good, affordable food for all. Most remarkably, he refused to allow young children to work in the factory, providing them instead with a decent education. He also banned all corporal punishment.

Owen was mill manager at New Lanark for a quarter of a century – from 1800 to 1825 – and there is no doubt that he would be delighted to see how his village has been preserved and restored. An award-winning visitor centre explains the importance of New Lanark and Owen's legacy.

Above: The Dunmore Pineapple is a folly par excellence – a witty and glorious piece of exotic 18th-century architecture.

DUNMORE PINEAPPLE
Near Falkirk, Stirling

Just a few miles south of Stirling can be found one of Scotland's most bizarre buildings: the Dunmore Pineapple. Built in 1761, at a time when pineapples and other exotic fruit were still rare and extremely costly, the 46-foot (14-metre) sandstone pineapple is actually a sort of gazebo, from where the Laird of Dunmore could look out across his gardens and land.

The pineapple forms part of a walled garden and reflects the fact that pineapples were being grown here in the 18th century – being able to cultivate such exotic fruit was a huge status symbol, and the stone pineapple would have announced the achievement to the world.

The Dunmore gardens, the Pineapple and the 16 acres (6.5 hectares) of surrounding land – the 'policies', as the land is known in Scotland – were given to the Landmark Trust by the Countess of Perth in 1974. They are now a rich haven for plants and wildlife, including the rare great-crested newt.

CULROSS

Near Kincardine, Fife

Most of us probably associate pretty villages with the rich lands of the south of England rather than with the rugged Scottish uplands, but hidden away here and there, Scotland has villages to match any England can offer. Perhaps the most beautiful of all is Culross.

Situated in a remote spot on the Firth of Forth, this perfect little settlement is the least spoiled example of a late 17th-century Scottish burgh (town). The beautifully restored and limewashed houses are architecturally typical of Scotland at that time: most have crows'-feet gables, pantile roofs and deeply set windows. The narrow cobbled streets – round which the houses seem almost to huddle for warmth – are just as they would have been when wealthy merchants walked them 300 years ago; at this time Culross was Scotland's wealthiest town. Best of all, there are no new developments to mar the scene.

The National Trust for Scotland owns many of the houses, including the splendid 'palace'. This was built for the 17th-century industrialist Sir George Bruce, and still has its delightful painted wooden ceilings. Sir George built an ironworks and mined coal from under the waters of the Firth. Furniture contemporary with the house has been added to provide a rare glimpse of what life would have been like in what was then a remote corner of the British Isles.

Another particularly interesting building in the village is The Study. Built in about 1600, it has a tower that would have allowed the original owners to look out across the sea for incoming ships: the town's prosperity was built on sea trade. Other houses almost certainly date back to the 1600s, and one has the date 1577 on its gable along with a brass plaque that reveals a later owner's sense of humour: 'In this spot in 1832 nothing happened!'

INCHCOLM ISLAND

Firth of Forth, Fife

A short journey across the Forth of Firth, over the stretch of water known intriguingly as Mortimer's Deep, will take you to one of the least known of Scotland's many islands.

In early medieval times, this bleak, windswept place was the sole preserve of perhaps just two or three monks linked to St Columba (c. AD 521–97), an Irish priest descended from the great kings of Ireland who is said to have brought Christianity to Scotland. The monks' tiny stone hut can still be seen.

In 1123, a great storm forced King Alexander I to take shelter on Inchcolm. Legend has it that he was so well looked after by the monks that he decided to build the monastery, whose remains can still be seen. Whatever the truth of its origins, we know that an Augustinian abbey was

Left: Culross Abbey is located on the edge of one of Britain's loveliest villages – Culross in Fife.

established here by 1223 and its remains are the best monastic ruins in Scotland. The great period of destruction that followed the Reformation was perhaps a little more thorough in Scotland than in England, thanks to the popular uptake of Calvinism.

Today, the ruins are the haunt of gulls and other seabirds, for the island is now uninhabited. It is a beautiful place to visit and trips can be made from either Aberdour or South Queensferry.

WADE'S BRIDGE
Aberfeldy, Perth & Kinross

Bonnie Prince Charlie used this extraordinary bridge in 1746 as he retreated north on his way to defeat at Culloden. It was the first bridge across Scotland's longest river – the Tay – and helped complete a network of roads built by one of Scotland's greatest enemies, General George Wade (1673–1748).

Wade's network of roads was designed to destroy the power of the clans by making it relatively easy for the forces of the English Crown to subdue any

Above: Wade's Bridge at Aberfeldy was used by Bonnie Prince Charlie on his way to the Battle of Culloden (1746), and it was the first bridge to be built across the River Tay.

disturbance or rebellion among the Highland Scots, such as the Jacobite rising of 1715. Wade was posted to Scotland in 1724 and his work there took nine years to complete; in that time he oversaw the construction of more than 250 miles (400km) of road and dozens of smaller bridges. Wade's Bridge at Aberfeldy, which is constructed from a beautiful grey chlorite schist taken from a local quarry, was so well made that it still carries traffic.

The bridge has five arches and is almost 400 feet (122 metres) long, a triumph of elegant 18th-century engineering in what was then a very remote region. William Adam, the greatest Scottish architect of the day, was employed to carry out the work. It took 400 men nearly a year to complete, at a total cost of £3596 (over £1 million today).

Wade's less great claim to fame is that he tragically used most of the stone from what was still a very well-preserved Hadrian's Wall to provide rubble and hard core for his road from Newcastle to Carlisle.

NELSON'S TOWER

Forres, Morayshire

Nelson's victory at the Battle of Trafalgar in 1805 was the cause of national celebrations on a quite unprecedented scale. Not content with feasting and fireworks, local communities collected funds to build permanent memorials to the great hero. Some memorials to Nelson, such as the column in London's Trafalgar Square, are famous throughout the world; others are less well known but equally fascinating. Among the best of these hidden monuments is Scotland's Nelson's Tower on Cluny Hill, Forres.

Ninety-six worn steps lead up through three floors to the top of the bizarre octagonal tower, from which there are splendid views north across the Moray Firth and south to the Grampians. There is an excellent permanent exhibition of local photographs and Nelson memorabilia on the top two floors, and a shop and reception on the ground floor.

The £610 it cost to build the tower was all raised locally, and, with an eye to future archaeologists, a parchment telling the story of Nelson's great victory and the building of the tower was placed under a foundation stone along with a few coins. It took six years to complete the 70-foot (21-metre) monument.

MAES HOWE TOMB

Near Kirkwall, Orkney

Neolithic remains exist all over Britain, but it is extremely rare to find those that show precisely how these distant ancestors built with wood or stone. One place where the extraordinary stone-masonry skills of Neolithic man can be clearly seen is at the Maes Howe chambered tomb in Orkney.

A 52-foot (16-metre) stone-lined passageway – precisely aligned with the position of the winter solstice – leads into the 5000-year-old tomb. Here, layers of slab stones cut with great precision rise gracefully to the corbelled ceiling, which is still complete. Small stones have been carefully shaped to fit into difficult places, and there is a sense of coherent planning throughout.

Left: The story behind the curious octagonal building that is Nelson's Tower is explained in a parchment that was buried beneath the building during its construction in the early 19th century.

When you leave Maes Howe it is easy to believe that you are still in the centre of an important Neolithic area, for just 10 minutes' walk away are the four ancient stones of Stenness. The tallest of these rises over 17 feet (5 metres), and their shadows fall virtually across the prehistoric village of Barnhouse, where some of the houses still have their internal features, including, in one, a stone fireplace carefully fixed in the centre of the floor.

DOUNBY CLICK MILL
Dounby, Orkney

Orkney is incredibly rich in prehistoric sites, from the extraordinary stone tomb at Maes Howe to the 5000-year-old village at Skara Brae, but less well known and of more recent date are the click mills. These were common across Orkney until relatively recent times. One of the best preserved, and the only one still in working order, is at Dounby. It was probably built towards the end of the 18th century or early in the 19th, and reveals a remarkably simple solution to the problem of harnessing power for grinding corn.

Without the powerful rivers of mainland Scotland, the islanders managed to find a way to harness what little water power – streams and becks – they had. They built low stone buildings above fast-flowing streams, and as water flowed through its natural channel beneath the building it would rush over the horizontally placed paddles of a specially designed wheel. An axle from the centre of this wheel passed up through the floor above and was fixed to the centre of a grindstone, which was turned by the force of the water

In many ways, these primitive mills were just one step up from grinding corn by hand. But they were effective and could produce enough corn for a few families. Their relatively small output explains the large number of click mill ruins that remain across the Scottish islands.

The mills' curious name comes from the noise made by a peg on the upper millstone, which was designed to strike the grainspout regularly so as to ensure a steady flow of grain into the hole in the centre of the stone.

Below: Dounby Click Mill is a monument to the ingenuity of the inhabitants of a remote island where there were few natural resources.

CONTACT DETAILS

Cornwall, Devon & Somerset

Land's End
Sennen, Penzance, Cornwall
TR19 7AA
Tel: 0870 458 0044
www.landsend-landmark.co.uk

Museum of Submarine Telegraphy
Eastern House, Porthcurno,
Cornwall TR19 6JX
Tel: (01736) 810966
www.porthcurno.org.uk

Minack Theatre
Porthcurno, Penzance, Cornwall
TR19 6JU
Tel: (01736) 810181
www.minack.com

Lanhydrock
Bodmin, Cornwall PL30 5AD
Tel: (01208) 265950
www.nationaltrust.org.uk

St Enodoc Church
Daymer Bay, near Rock, Cornwall
www.rockinfo.co.uk/daymer/
stenochc.html

Tintagel Visitor Centre
Bossiney Road Car Park,
Tintagel, Cornwall PL34 0AJ
Tel: (01840) 779084
www.tintagelweb.co.uk

Buckland Abbey
Yelverton, Devon PL20 6EY
Tel: (01822) 853607
www.nationaltrust.org.uk

Buckfast Abbey
Buckfast Abbey, Buckfastleigh,
Devon TQ11 0EE
Tel: (01364) 645550
www.buckfast.org.uk

Arlington Court
near Barnstaple, Devon
EX31 4LP
Tel: (01271) 850296
www.nationaltrust.org.uk

Heddon Valley
Parracombe, Barnstaple, Devon
EX31 4PY
Tel: (01598) 763402
www.nationaltrust.org.uk

Brean Down
Brean, Somerset
Tel: (01934) 844518
www.nationaltrust.org.uk

Burrow Mump
Isle of Athelney, near Taunton,
Somerset

Muchelney Abbey
Muchelney, near Langport,
Somerset TA10 0DG
Tel: (01458) 250664
www.english-heritage.org.uk

Dorset, Wiltshire & Hampshire

Golden Cap
near Bridport, Dorset
www.nationaltrust.org.uk

Eggardon Hill
Bridport, Dorset

The Smith's Arms
Godmanstone, Dorchester,
Dorset DT2 7AQ
Tel: (01300) 341236

St Laurence's Church
Bradford-on-Avon, Wiltshire

The Peto Garden
Iford Manor, Bradford-on-Avon,
Wiltshire BA15 2BA
Tel: (01225) 863146
www.ifordmanor.co.uk

Caen Hill Locks
Devizes, Wiltshire

Silbury Hill
Near Marlborough, Wiltshire

Cherhill Down
Near Calne, Wiltshire

Maud Heath's Causeway
East Tytherington to
Chippenham, Wiltshire
www.walkscene.co.uk/England/
Wiltshire/Maud1.htm

Malmesbury Abbey
Malmesbury, Wiltshire
SN16 9BA
Tel: (01666) 826666
www.malmesburyabbey.com

North Meadow National Nature Reserve
Cricklade, Wiltshire SN10 2RT
Tel: (01380) 726344
www.english-nature.org.uk

Pepperbox Hill
Near Salisbury, Wiltshire
www.nationaltrust.org.uk

Mottisfont Abbey
near Romsey, Hampshire
SO51 0LP
Tel: (01794) 340757
www.nationaltrust.org.uk

Bembridge Maritime Museum and Shipwreck Centre
Sherborne Street, Bembridge,
Isle of Wight
Tel: (01983) 87222
www.wightindex.com

Worcestershire, Herefordshire, Gloucestershire, Warwickshire & Oxfordshire

Clent Hills
National Trust, High Harcourt
Farm, Romsley, Halesowen,
West Midlands B62 0NQ
Tel: (01562) 711023
www.nationaltrust.org.uk

Croft Castle
near Leominster, Herefordshire
HR6 9PW
Tel: (01568) 780246
www.nationaltrust.org.uk

Lower Brockhampton
Greenfields, Bringsty,
Worcestershire WR6 5TB
Tel: (01885) 488099
www.nationaltrust.org.uk

Owlpen Manor
near Uley, Gloucestershire
GL11 5BZ
Tel: (01453) 860261
www.owlpen.com

St Mary's Priory Church
Deerhurst, Gloucestershire
GL19 4BX
Tel: (01452) 780880

Cleeve Hill
near Cheltenham,
Gloucestershire GL52 3PR

Stanway House
near Winchcombe,
Gloucestershire GL54 5PQ
Tel: (01386) 584469
www.stanwayfountain.co.uk

Hick's Almshouses
Chipping Campden,
Gloucestershire
www.nationaltrust.org.uk

The Fleece Inn
Bretforton, near Evesham,
Worcestershire WR11 5JE
Tel: (01386) 831173
www.thefleeceinn.co.uk

Packwood House
Lapworth, Solihull, West
Midlands B94 6AT
Tel: (01564) 783294
www.nationaltrust.org.uk

Swalcliffe Barn
Shipston Road, Swalcliffe, near
Banbury, Oxfordshire
Tel: (01295) 788278

Great Tew
Near Chipping Norton,
Oxfordshire

St Oswald's Church
Widford, near Swinbrook,
Oxfordshire

Wayland's Smithy
Off B4507, Ashbury, Swindon,
Wiltshire

**Mapledurham House &
Watermill**
Mapledurham, Reading
RG4 7TR
Tel: (01189) 723350
www.mapledurham.co.uk

Stonor Park
Henley-on-Thames, Oxfordshire
RG9 6HF
Tel: (01491) 638587
www.stonor.com

London & the home counties

Geffrye Museum
136 Kingsland Road,
Shoreditch, London E2 8EA
Tel: (020) 7739 9893
www.geffrye-museum.org.uk

Kensal Green Cemetery
The General Cemetery
Company, Harrow Road,
London W10 4RA
www.kensalgreen.co.uk

Linley Sambourne House
18 Stafford Terrace, Kensington,
London W8 7BH
Tel: (020) 7602 3316
www.rbkc.gov.uk/
linleysambournehouse/
general/default.asp

The George Inn
77 Borough High Street,
Southwark, London SE1 1NH
Tel: (020) 7407 2056

London Wetland Centre
The Wildfowl and Wetlands
Trust, Queen Elizabeth's Walk,
Barnes, London SW13 9WT
Tel: (020) 8409 4400
www.wwt.org.uk

Cardinal's Wharf
Bankside, London SE1

Berry Bros & Rudd
3 St James's Street, London
SW1A 1EG
Tel: 0870 900 4300
www.bbr.com

Lock & Co. Hatters
6 St James's Street, London
SW1A 1EF
Tel: (020) 7930 8874
www.lockhatters.co.uk

St Mary's Church
Aldworth, Berkshire
www.aldworth.info/~church/
index2.html

Finchampstead Ridges
Finchampstead, Berskhire
www.finchampstead-pc.gov.uk

Bekonscot Model Village
Warwick Road, Beaconsfield,
Buckinghamshire HP9 2PL
Tel: (01494) 672919
www.bekonscot.org.uk

Hellfire Caves
West Wycombe Hill Road, West
Wycombe, Buckinghamshire
HP14 3AJ
Tel: (01494) 533739
www.hellfirecaves.co.uk

Coombe Hill
Wendover, Buckinghamshire
www.thamesvalleyguide.co.uk/to
_do/walks/coombe_hill.htm

Waddesdon Manor
Waddesdon, near Aylesbury,
Buckinghamshire HP18 0JH
Tel: (01296) 653226
www.waddesdon.org.uk

Claydon House
Middle Claydon, near
Buckingham, Buckinghamshire
MK18 2EY
Tel: (01296) 730349
www.nationaltrust.org.uk

Ivinghoe Beacon
Chiltern Hills, Buckinghamshire
www.english-heritage.org.uk

Bromham Mill
Bridge End, Bromham,
Bedfordshire MK43 8LP
Tel: (01234) 824330

The Swiss Garden
Old Warden Aerodrome,
Old Warden, Biggleswade,
Bedfordshire SG18 9ER
Tel: (01767) 627666

**Flitton Church and the De
Grey Mausoleum**
3 Highfield Road, Flitton,
Bedfordshire MK45 5EB
Tel: (01525) 860094
www.english-heritage.org.uk

Wrest Park Gardens
Silsoe, Bedfordshire MK45 4HS
Tel: (01525) 860152

Welwyn Roman Baths
Welwyn Bypass, Welwyn,
Hertfordshire AL6 9HT
Tel: (01707) 271362

Shaw's Corner
Ayot St Lawrence, near Welwyn,
Hertfordshire AL6 9BX
Tel: (01438) 820307
www.nationaltrust.org.uk

Gardens of the Rose
Chiswell Green, St Albans,
Hertfordshire AL2 3NR
Tel: (01727) 850461

Fighting Cocks
16 Abbey Mill Lane, St Albans,
Hertfordshire AL3 4HE
Tel: (01727) 865830

Surrey, Sussex & Kent

**Chatley Heath Semaphore
Tower**
Old Lane, Chatley Heath,
Surrey
Tel: (01372) 458822

Headley Common
Near Dorking, Surrey

**Church of St Peter and
St Paul**
Church Lane, Chaldon, Surrey
CR3 5AL
Tel: (020) 8660 4015

Holmbury Hill
near Holmbury St Mary, Surrey

Leith Hill
near Coldharbour, Surrey
Tel: (01306) 711777
www.nationaltrust.org.uk

Parham House and Gardens
Parham Park, near Pulborough,
West Sussex RH20 4HS
Tel: (01903) 744888
www.parhaminsussex.co.uk

St Botolph's Church
Church Lane, Coldwaltham,
Pulborough, West Sussex
RH20 1LW

Cissbury Ring
Near Findon, West Sussex

Chyngton Farm
Chyngton Lane, Alfriston,
East Sussex
www.nationaltrust.org.uk

Jack Fuller's Pyramid
Brightling, East Sussex

Bateman's
Burwash, Etchingham,
East Sussex TN19 7DS
Tel: (01435) 882302
www.nationaltrust.org.uk

The Mermaid Inn
Rye, East Sussex TN31 7EY
Tel: (01797) 223065
www.mermaidinn.com

St Augustine's Church
Brookland, Kent TN26 2DB
Tel: (01233) 758250

Derek Jarman's Garden
Prospect Cottage, Dungeness,
Kent

St Leonard's Church
Oak Walk, Hythe, Kent
CT21 5DN
Tel: (01303) 262370
www.stleonardschurch.com

The Grand Shaft
South Military Road,
Dover, Kent
Tel: (01304) 201200

Cambridgeshire, Essex, Suffolk & Norfolk

Flag Fen Bronze Age Centre
The Droveway, Northey Road,
Peterborough, Cambridgeshire
PE6 7QJ
Tel: (01733) 313414
www.flagfen.com

Wicken Fen
Lode Lane, Wicken, Ely,
Cambridgeshire CB7 5XP
Tel: (01353) 720274
www.wicken.org.uk

Anglesey Abbey
Lode, Cambridgeshire CB5 9EJ
Tel: (01223) 810080
www.nationaltrust.org.uk/
angleseyabbey

Wimpole Hall and Farm
Arrington, Royston,
Cambridgeshire SG8 0BW
Tel: (01223) 207257
www.wimpole.org

St Andrew's Church
Greensted Road, Chipping
Ongar, Essex CM5 9LA
Tel: (01277) 364694

Thrift Wood
Bicknacre, near Maldon, Essex
www.essexwt.org.uk

St Peter on the Wall
Bradwell-on-Sea, Essex
www.bradwellchapel.org

Layer Marney Tower
Colchester, Essex CO5 9US
Tel: (01206) 330784
www.layermarneytower.co.uk

Tattingstone Wonder
Tattingstone, Suffolk

Ickworth House
Ickworth, The Rotunda,
Horringer, Bury St Edmunds,
Suffolk IP29 5QE
Tel: (01284) 735270
www.nationaltrust.org.uk

The Nutshell
17 The Traverse, Bury
St Edmunds, Suffolk IP33 1BJ
Tel: (01284) 764867

Welney Wildfowl Reserve
Hundred Foot Bank, Welney,
Norfolk PE14 9TN
Tel: (01353) 860711
www.wwt.org.uk

**Church of St Peter and
St Paul**
Salle, Norfolk

Blickling Hall
Blickling, Norwich, Norfolk
NR11 6NF
Tel: (01263) 738030
www.nationaltrust.org.uk

Walsingham Abbey Grounds
Common Place, Little
Walsingham, Norfolk
NR22 6BP
Tel: (01328) 820510

Blakeney Point
Norfolk Coast Office
Friary Farm
Cley Road, Blakeney
Norfolk NR25 7NW
Tel: (01263) 740241
www.nationaltrust.org.uk

Northamptonshire, Rutland, Leicestershire, Nottinghamshire & Lincolnshire

Church of the Holy Sepulchre
Guildhall Road, Northampton
Tel: (01604) 838400

Eleanor Cross
Jct West Street/Bridge Street,
Geddington, Northamptonshire

The Clipsham Yews
Clipsham, Rutland

**Loughborough Bell Foundry
and Museum**
John Taylor Bellfounders Ltd,
Freehold Street, Loughborough,
Leicestershire LE11 1AR
Tel: (01509) 233414
www.taylorbells.co.uk

Southwell Workhouse
Upton Road, Southwell,
Nottinghamshire NG25 0PT
Tel: (01636) 817250
www.nationaltrust.org.uk

Upton Hall Time Museum
British Horological Institute,
Upton Hall, Upton, Newark-on-
Trent, Nottinghamshire
NG23 5TE
Tel: (01636) 813795
www.bhi.co.uk/tour/
uptonhal.htm

Laxton
Near Newark-on-Trent,
Nottinghamshire

Clumber Park
The Estate Office, Clumber
Park, Worksop, Nottinghamshire
S80 3AZ
Tel: (01909) 476592
www.nationaltrust.org.uk

Mr Straw's House
7 Blyth Grove, Worksop,
Nottinghamshire S81 0JG
Tel: (01909) 482380
www.nationaltrust.org.uk

Gainsborough Old Hall
Parnell Street, Gainsborough,
Lincolnshire DN21 2NB
Tel: (01427) 612669
http://gainsborougholdhall.
freewebspace.com/

The Jew's House
15 The Strait, Lincoln,
Lincolnshire LN2 1JD
Tel: (01522) 524851

Tattershall Castle
Tattershall, Lincoln,
Lincolnshire LN4 4LR
Tel: (01526) 342543
www.nationaltrust.org.uk

Sibsey Trader Windmill
Sibsey, Lincolnshire
Tel: (01205) 750036
www.sibsey.fsnet.co.uk/
Trader_Windmill_Sibsey.htm

Maud Foster Mill
Willoughby Road, Boston,
Lincolnshire PE21 9EG
Tel: (01205) 352188

Shropshire, West Midlands, Staffordshire, Cheshire & Derbyshire

The Long Mynd
Near Chruch Stretton,
Shropshire

Wenlock Edge
Near Chruch Stretton,
Shropshire

Red House Glass Cone
High Street, Wordsley,
Stourbridge, West Midlands
DY8 4AZ
Tel: (01384) 812750
www.redhousecone.co.uk

Bournville
Near Birmingham, West
Midlands
www.bournville-web.net

Soho House
Soho Avenue (off Soho Road),
Handsworth, Birmingham
B18 5LB
Tel: (0121) 554 9122
www.bmag.org.uk/sohohouse

Cannock Chase
near Cannock, Staffordshire
www.cannockchasedc.gov.uk

Gladstone Pottery Museum
Uttoxeter Road, Longton,
Stoke-on-Trent, Staffordshire
ST3 1PQ
Tel: (01782) 319232
www.2002.stoke.gov.uk/
museums/gladstone

Cheddleton Flint Mill
Leek Road, Cheddleton, near
Leek, Staffordshire ST13 7HL
Tel: (01782) 502907
www.ex.ac.uk/~akoutram/
cheddleton-mill

The Salt Museum
162 London Road, Northwich,
Cheshire CW9 8AB
Tel: (01606) 41331
www.saltmuseum.org.uk

Alderley Edge
near Macclesfield, Cheshire

Buxton Opera House
Water Street, Buxton,
Derbyshire SK17 6XN
Tel: (01298) 72050
www.buxton-opera.co.uk

Mam Tor
Castleton, The Peak District
National Park, Derbyshire
Tel: (01629) 813227

Speedwell Cavern
Winnats Pass, Castleton Hope
Valley, Derbyshire S33 8WA
Tel: (01433) 620512
www.speedwellcavern.co.uk

Eyam
Derbyshire
www.derbyshireuk.net/
eyam.html

Calke Abbey
Ticknall, Derby, Derbyshire
DE73 7LE
Tel: (01332) 863822
www.nationaltrust.org.uk

Cumbria, Lancashire, Yorkshire & Northumberland

Printing House Museum
102 Main Street, Cockermouth,
Cumbria CA13 9LX
Tel: (01900) 824984

Eskdale Watermill
Boot, Eskdale, Cumbria
CA19 1TG
Tel: (01946) 723335

Duddon Valley
Cumbria
www.duddonvalley.co.uk

Heysham Head
Near Morecambe, Lancashire
www.nationaltrust.org.uk

Hall-i'-th'-Wood
Green Way, off Crompton Way,
Bolton, Lancashire BL1 8UA
Tel: (01204) 332370
www.bolton.org.uk/
hallithwood.html

Barton Swing Aqueduct
Barton-upon-Irwell, Trafford,
Greater Manchester

Piece Hall
Halifax, West Yorkshire
HX1 1RE
Tel: (01422) 358087
www.piecehall.info

Saltaire
near Shipley, West Yorkshire
www.saltaire.yorks.com

Bridestones Moor
near Whitby, Pickering,
North Yorkshire YO62 7JL
Tel: (01751) 431693
www.nationaltrust.org.uk

Stephenson's Cottage
Wylam NE41 8BP
Tel: (01661) 853457
www.nationaltrust.org.uk

Allen Banks
Bardon Mill, Hexham,
Northumberland NE47 7BU
Tel: (01434) 344218
www.nationaltrust.org.uk

Beadnell Limekilns
Beadnell, Northumberland
www.beadnell.org/history/

Bamburgh Castle and Beaches
Bamburgh, Northumberland
NE69 7DF
Tel: (01668) 214515
www.bamburghcastle.com

Wales

Conwy
www.conwy.gov.uk

Newborough Beach
Newborough, Anglesey

Portmeirion
near Porthmadog, Gwynedd
Tel: (01766) 770000
www.portmeirion.wales.com

Dinas Island
Near Fishguard, Pembrokeshire
www.pembrokeshirecoast.org.uk

St Govan's Chapel
Near Bosherston, Pembrokeshire

Aberglasney Gardens
Llangathen, Carmarthenshire
SA32 8QH
Tel: (01558) 668998
www.aberglasney.org

Aberdeunant
Taliaris, Llandeilo,
Carmarthenshire SA19 6DL
Tel: (01558) 650177
www.nationaltrust.org.uk

Joseph Parry's Cottage
4 Chapel Row, Georgetown,
Merthyr Tydfil, Mid Glamorgan
CF48 1BN
Tel: (01685) 721858

Big Pit National Mining Museum
Blaenafon, Torfaen NP4 9XP
Tel: (01495) 790311
www.nmgw.ac.uk/bigpit/

Castell Coch
Castle Hill, Tongwynlais, Cardiff
CF15 7JS
Tel: (029) 2081 0101
www.cadw.wales.gov.uk

The Kymin
Monmouth, Monmouthshire
NP25 3SE
Tel: (01600) 719241
www.nationaltrust.org.uk

The Begwns
Near Hay-on-Wye, Radnorshire

Scotland

Bowmore Distillery
Isle of Islay, Argyll & Bute
PA43 7GS
Tel: (01496) 8104411
www.bowmorescotch.com

Crossraguel Abbey
Maybole, Ayrshire KA19 8HQ
Tel: (01655) 883113
www.historic-scotland.gov.uk

New Lanark
South Lanarkshire ML11 9DB
Tel: (01555) 661345
www.newlanark.org

Dunmore Pineapple
Dunmore House,
near Falkirk, Stirling
Tel: (01628) 825925

Culross
near Kincardine, Fife
www.culross.org

Inchcolm Island
Firth of Forth, Fife
www.historic-scotland.gov.uk

Wade's Bridge
Aberfeldy, Perth & Kinross

Nelson's Tower
Forres, Moray
Tel: (01309) 673701
www.moray.gov.uk/museums/
facilities/nelson.html

Maes Howe Tomb
Near Kirkwall, Orkney
Tel: (01856) 761606
www.historic-scotland.gov.uk

Dounby Click Mill
Dounby, Orkney
Tel: (01856) 841815
www.historic-scotland.gov.uk

INDEX